between the lines and spaces

between the
lines and spaces

Christian artists share the stories behind their songs

BARTON GREEN

Standard®
PUBLISHING
Bringing The Word to Life

Cincinnati, Ohio

© 2006 Barton Green.

Published by Standard Publishing, Cincinnati, Ohio. A division of Standex International Corporation. All rights reserved. No part of this book may be reproduced in any form, except for brief quotations in reviews, without the written permission of the publisher. The Power of Christian Music™ is a trademark of Standard Publishing.

Printed in the USA.

Project editor: Laura Derico

Cover design: Robert Glover

Interior design: Ahaa! Design

All stories are written by Barton Green, as told to him and provided by the respective artists.

Photo credits: Cover/Scott Ryan, p.15/adeleredingphotography.com, p. 27/Juan Pont Lezica, p. 35/Courtesy of Universal South, p. 47/Courtesy of Margaret Becker Productions/CinemationMedia, p. 57/Russ Harrington, p. 69/Courtesy of Thomas-Vasquez Entertainment, p. 79/Courtesy of Anthony Burger Productions, p. 89/Russell Baer/LA, p. 99/Courtesy of Word Entertainment, p. 111/Kristen Barlow, p. 123/Courtesy of Rocketown Records, p. 133/Laughlin Photography, p. 141/Michael Gomez, p. 153/Courtesy of Ken Steorts, p. 163/Marty Funderburk, p. 177/Courtesy of Michael Peterson, p. 187/Courtesy of Wayne Kirkpatrick, p. 197/Courtesy of Word Entertainment, p. 209/Courtesy of Word Entertainment, p. 224/Darla Jackson.

ISBN 0-7847-1656-0

12 11 10 09 08 07 06   9 8 7 6 5 4 3 2 1

Words make you think a thought.

Music makes you feel a feeling.

A song makes you feel a thought.

—E.Y. Harburg, lyricist

Contents

I've spent my entire adult life surrounded by songwriters. I am one (for thirty years), I married one (five-time Grammy Award winner Russ Taff), and I've co-written and toured with a whole bunch of 'em. Suffice it to say, I have the utmost respect for both the art *and* the craft of pairing words with music. It's incredibly difficult to find a new way to say something timeless—with a bridge and a chorus!

But the songs that have meant the most to me, the ones that have resonated inside and provided an indelible soundtrack to my life, are the ones that feel *real*—like they couldn't help but be written, like they were a message in a bottle from God, just for me. Such rare songs are a gift to both the writer and the listener and, in the case of this book, readers too.

What Barton Green has managed to do so beautifully in this collection is to track down the real stories behind some of the most real songs ever written. He spent time with these artists and writers, getting *between the lines and spaces*, absorbing the essence of their private experiences and inspiration. Using his own masterful gifts as a storyteller, he makes the songs come alive and gives them a context, seamlessly weaving the lyrics throughout the narrative.

In a way that I have never seen more accurately portrayed, Bart chronicles that painful, poignant perfection a writer *feels* when he knows he has fully expressed what God gave him for that song, that day, that moment in time.

It's a personal process, an individual journey, but the end result is universal—the truth always is.

Tori Taff
Nashville, Tennessee

Laney's Lullaby

Motion madness, vertigo, being seasick in the car—that pretty much describes how I spent my childhood summer vacations with the family.

Growing up in the South, it was a given that any journey extending more than fifty miles would in some way include a trek through the mountains over winding roller coaster roads. And among the more horrendous of these E-ticket rides were the trails that meandered through the Appalachian range of Kentucky and West Virginia.

The unexpected curves, hairpin turns and the blur of scenery flying by my window always had me crawling over the car's front seat to stretch out in the back, where my grandmother often sat. Resting my spinning head in her lap, I would close my eyes tight and try to shut out the world flying by. After a moment I'd feel the gentle caress of my grandmother's small fingers combing through my hair, and the rumble of the road would fade as she softly hummed a little tune.

She was the quiet one in the family.

Both my father and grandfather were ministers, capable of holding an audience's attention with the mere sound of their spoken thoughts. My mother, a gifted organist, could make a cathedral come alive. And my younger brother, who would later become a Broadway star, could dissipate the gloom in the room with just a phrase from his then soprano voice. But my little grandmother could do all of this and more, with just the presence of her quiet strength.

She never said much, she didn't have to; her silent, selfless acts spoke louder than words. Laney, as we called her, had a way of stepping into our lives, giving us the benefit of her wisdom, her grand mothering, without intrusion. She was as strong and silent as an oak, as inviting as a sprawling shade tree. Though her acts were quietly performed, it is the sound of her rarely-heard voice, in the backseat of our car, that still echoes in my memory.

We traveled a lot during my childhood and I spent many of those road trips lying down in the backseat, listening to Laney's lullaby. Over time, her melody would grow into a little song and she would compose impromptu lyrics to fit whatever state we were in—on the map or otherwise. But, if I was in the backseat, we were most likely in the mountains.

We're on a mountain in the sky

Up in the clouds way up high

But there's a city drawing nigh

Over the mountain in the sky

Her whispered, melodic words were few but profound. Although she was the quiet one, to me Laney's simple song was as inspiring as one of my grandfather's sermons.

We're on a mountain in the sky

Up in the clouds way up high

Reclining in the backseat, I came to understand that there's no way to avoid the mountain. Life is an uphill struggle, at best, with unpredictable twists, cloud-shrouded turns, and hairpin curves. I can close my eyes and wish that the world would just stop, but there is no way around the mountain. It must be climbed.

But though Laney's lullaby never sugar-coated the state of my surroundings, her lyric was not just a lesson, but also an encouragement.

But there's a city drawing nigh

Over the mountain in the sky

Listening to those words, I knew if I would just hold on, that not far down the road, just over the mountain, there would be a city; a rest stop where we could pull over and stretch our legs, and where the family could grab a bite to eat. Once we made it to the rest stop, all of the maddening motion on the twisted road would be forgotten.

Today, I am certain that when I have finally climbed the mountain and negotiated my own way through every twist and turn, I, too, will see the City—that ultimate rest stop. With my eyes wide open, having moved beyond the vertigo of this world, I'll pick up the pace a little because I know old friends and family will already be there, getting ready for a bite to eat. Somewhere in the middle of this bunch, I'll spy the tall Texan frame of my grandfather emerging with open arms. And hanging onto one of those arms will be a little wisp of a thing, smiling from ear to ear.

After dinner we'll all stretch our legs, take a walk down by the river, and find a patch of shade trees. Under their branches we'll sit, sing, and laugh about the journey, forgetting all about the twists and turns of the road.

And, once more, I'll rest my head in my grandmother's lap and enjoy the gentle caress of her fingers combing through my hair.

This volume is affectionately dedicated to Nellie Boman Lane— "Laney." Just as I was completing the final pages of this collection, she concluded the last chapter of her story. Laney's quiet strength taught me the value of a few well-chosen words. Her long, selfless, well-lived life is a melody I will never forget.

A paragraph is one idea fully formed,
with a period at the end.

Life is not a paragraph. A life never reaches its completion. There may be a pause, when the soul leaves the body, but there is no ultimate finality. If anything, life is a line of poetry, a rhythmic phrase; a repeated lyric that can mean different things according to when and where it turns up in the song.

In the compositions of today's inspirational artists, every lyric is about the same life. The names may change, the plots may vary, but the lead character is always the same. Peel back every line, like an onion, and another story will appear. Move to the next verse and another facet of his character will emerge. Each rhyme is a play on the Word that became flesh. Each phrase is another tale of how he moves among us.

The lyrics found in these pages are chosen from among the most intuitive compositions of our time. Taken as a whole, each song is moving, amazing. But between the lines and spaces of the music, many facets of truth can be found. Pull back the layers and you will find parallel tales, behind-the-scenes epochs, and intimate vignettes from the composers themselves.

Life is not a paragraph. It is an endless story . . .
punctuated by wonders!

Steven Curtis Chapman

Since beginning his career in 1987, Steven Curtis Chapman has sold more than ten million records and recorded fifteen projects with Sparrow Records.His most recent studio record, titled *All Things New*, was released in September, 2004. He also appeared on the soundtrack for the 2005 Disney blockbuster *The Chronicles of Narnia: The Lion, the Witch and the Wardrobe*. He's received five Grammy Awards, an American Music Award, fifty Dove Awards (more than any other artist to date), and has recorded forty-four No. 1 radio hits. His platinum and gold albums include *Speechless*, *Heaven in the Real World*, *Declaration*, *Greatest Hits*, *Music of Christmas*, *Signs of Life*, *The Great Adventure*, *More to This Life*, and *For the Sake of the Call*.

Born and raised in Paducah, Kentucky, Steven is married to Mary Beth, and they have six children ranging from twenty-something to toddler age—Emily, Caleb, Will Franklin, Shaohannah, Stevey Joy, and Maria Sue. The youngest three daughters were adopted from China, and Chapman and his family are now some of the country's leading advocates for adoption. They have developed an organization, Shaohannah's Hope, which provides information and financial grants to families wishing to adopt. Steven is an advisory board member of the Congressional Coalition on Adoption Institute (CCAI), and he and his wife have also co-authored children's picture books in a series about adoption, published by Tommy Nelson Publishing.

Just Another Day

It was the end of another beginning. The morning rush hour was winding down. The mad dash to beat the first period bell was over, at least for another day.

As I turned out of the school parking lot, the road back home felt a little like victory lane. Driving my kids to school was a lap of the human race I rarely got the chance to run. My usual daily dash was beating the clock to make my next concert. It felt good to be home, part of that rural routine. Getting back into the cadence of real life was comforting, fulfilling; like finding just the right rhythm for a song.

As I drove, passing school buses and soccer-mom vans, I realized it would be a long time before the Chapman family shuttle would go out of business. With a clan that ranges from just-out-of-diapers to just-into-college, the road between the world and our home would be well traveled for many years to come. I pondered this with a smile, and my drifting mind rolled down the road, envisioning the many birthdays, graduations, and weddings yet to be.

But like most daydreams, mine were interrupted by reality.

On the road just ahead, a tangible vision of the future appeared. The sight within the frame of my windshield was familiar but unexpected; inching toward me was a long, meandering line of headlights. Although the morning sun was peeking over the Tennessee hills, a double row of white circular beams shined. It was as if the slow-moving caravan was feeling its way through the darkest of nights.

Compelled by reverence and tradition, I pulled off onto the shoulder. And in the relative silence of my idling car, I watched the solemn funeral procession pass.

Through the windows I could see glimpses of bowed heads, fleeting glances of sober eyes, and handkerchiefs hiding from view the full expression of loss. This was the last road they would travel with their loved one. It was the end of another beginning.

I had no idea who the solemn parade was for. It could have been anyone familiar with this road: a rush-hour bus driver, a schedule-keeping soccer mom, or a child teenager with daydreams of coming birthdays, graduations, and weddings. Watching the slow procession, I was reminded that there are no guarantees. The human race has no standard number of laps. The finish line could be just around the corner, or a few hundred more trips around the world.

As the limousines slowly filed by, I found myself wondering how the departed had spent that final day. Was it surrounded by family, enjoying their rural routine? Was it stuck in rush-hour traffic, trying to beat the clock? Or, like me, was the daydream interrupted by an unexpected reminder of reality?

What if this is my last day?

Any other time the question would've been rhetorical, whimsical, like "What if I had a billion dollars?" But as I gazed out the window at my proximity to that hearse, the notion of "the end" appeared alarmingly close, and in that moment the question became real, relevant.

What if this is my last day?

Glimpsing the casket through the hearse window, I wondered if the same question had crossed the occupant's mind, and if so, did it change the way those final hours were spent? No one can know the answer this side of Heaven, but there are only two real options. Either that soul lived life the rhetorical way—never taking the question seriously until it was too late, or left this world the Rudd way, ever mindful that each day could be the last.

As my grandfather's face flashed across my mind, I found myself hoping that the departed had died the way Rubel Rudd had lived.

Grandpa Rudd knew what it was like to face the daily possibility of death. Growing up in the wake of the depression, when food was scarce and disease ran rampant, he managed to beat the odds and reach relative manhood in time for World War II. After enduring a grueling boot camp, Rubel found himself in the thick of the fight. But though death constantly surrounded him, and despite being wounded in battle (for which he earned a purple heart), he fulfilled his purpose, stayed the course, and did his job. He continued to live every day to the fullest, like it was his last. Ever examining his own actions, he took his life's work seriously and consistently completed every task on his to-do list, right up until his last day, eighty-eight years after his first.

Watching the procession, thinking back to Grandpa's own parade just a few weeks before, I couldn't imagine him being surprised by anything, especially that final lap. On his last day I just can't see him tossing his to-do list out the window and spending his final hours rethinking his life. Although his passing caught me off guard, like a caravan of headlights on a sunny morning, I have no doubt that Grandpa was prepared, ever ready. I imagine him going about his business like it was just another day, checking off each event in his day planner, till everything was done, complete, and ultimately finished.

Eventually the last limousine passed, and I put my idling car in gear. In the rearview mirror I watched a double row of red taillights flash in lazy, random succession; the caravan was in no hurry. The mad dash to beat the first period bell was over, at least for the departed. As for the rest of us . . .

Pulling back onto the road, I realized that my kids were not the only ones who had made it to school on time. Everything we see and experience is a classroom. And rolling down the road between the world and my home, I considered the lesson. I thought about the cadence of my life and how so much of it was spent finding the right rhythm for a song. I mused about my constant daily dash to beat the clock, to make the next concert, and how so precious little of my time was available to be a part of my family's rural routine.

How would I spend my last day?

As I envisioned the many birthdays, graduations, and weddings I may miss, the vibrations of the wheels on the pavement began to pulse like a metronome, like a song.

If this should be my last day on this earth

How then shall I live?

As the words began to flow, I felt the familiar need to write them down, and my foot grew heavier on the accelerator.

If this should be the last day that I have

Aware of both the forming words and my sudden reason to get home, I realized I was actually answering the question; I was on the job, fulfilling my purpose. If this was my last day, I wasn't tossing my to-do list out the window; I was trying to get to paper and pen.

Before I breathe the air of heaven

Let me live it with abandon . . .

The faster the words came, the tighter I gripped the steering wheel. Mindful of the center line and the boundaries of my journey, I considered the importance of staying the course, not just within my lane, but on that ultimate road between the world and my heavenly home.

If tomorrow comes to find me

Looking in the face of Jesus

Will I hear him say the words "Well done"?

Taking my kids to school that morning, I got an education. I learned the answer to the query that has been put to everyone who has ever lived—the same non-rhetorical question that a young student once nervously posed to his professor, the great Martin Luther.

"What would you do today, if you knew it was your last?"

Luther thought for a moment, then turned to the student with the same air of resolve his adversaries had come to know. "Well, I would go home and plant a tree."

Looking at the Reformation leader sideways, the young scholar wrinkled his brow. "Plant a tree? What is the spiritual significance of that?"

"The significance?" Luther replied. "None. The tree is on my list of things to do today. If you are living your life ever ready to meet your maker, then your last day should be no different from any other."

Stepping into the house, I threw my keys on the counter, picked up a pad and pen, and recorded the morning's events in verse.

⤲

I pull over to the side of the road

And I watch the cars pass me by

The headlights and black limousines

Tell me someone is saying good-bye

I bow my head and I whisper a prayer

"Father, comfort their broken hearts"

And as I drive away there's a thought

That I cannot escape

No, I cannot escape this thought

⤲

As I scribbled the words onto the page, it felt comforting, fulfilling. And I realized this was my purpose, my work. My songs were seeds—my version of planting trees. If I live my life Rubel Rudd's way—prepared, ever ready, ever mindful not only of birthdays and weddings, but of the funerals yet to be—I will never be caught off guard by what may come down the road. Like Grandpa, the cadence of my life will be a lesson for my children, no matter how long the Chapman family shuttle stays in business.

And when my last day comes, it will be no different from any other; for when that final bell tolls, it will merely be a sign that I was prepared and I made it to my next class . . . on time.

⚜ Prayer ⚜

No more daydreams. Don't let me live a rhetorical life. Let every page of my day planner be as relevant as the last five minutes of my calendar. When I reach the end of the road, and you review my to-do list, let me hear the words "Well done," that I may be worthy of that next classroom—that endless day, far brighter than the Tennessee sun.

> I have fought the good fight; I have finished the race; I have redeemed my pledge; I look forward to the prize that is waiting for me, the prize I have earned. The Lord, the judge whose award never goes amiss, will grant it to me when that day comes.
>
> 2 TIMOTHY 4:6-8 *(KNOX)*

Last Day on Earth

‹ BY STEPHEN CURTIS CHAPMAN ›

I pull over to the side of the road
And I watch the cars pass me by
The headlights and black limousines
Tell me someone is saying good-bye
I bow my head and I whisper a prayer
"Father, comfort their broken hearts"
And as I drive away there's a
    thought
That I cannot escape

No I cannot escape this thought
I can't get away

If this should be my last day on
    this earth
How then shall I live?
If this should be the last day that
    I have
Before I breathe the air of heaven
Let me live it with abandon to
The only thing that remains
After my last day, here on earth

If this should be my last day here
    on earth
If this should be my last day here
    on earth
If this should be my last, last day
    here on earth
And if tomorrow comes to find me
Looking in the face of Jesus
Will I hear him say the words
    "Well done"?

If this should be my last day on
    this earth
How then shall I live?
If this should be the last day that
    I have
Before I breathe the air of heaven
Let me live it with abandon to
The only One that remains
After my last day
Here on earth

If this should be my last day
Here on earth
If this should be my last
My last day here on earth
'Cause this could be my last
This could be my last
This could be my last day

Susan Ashton

Susan Rae Hill was born in Irving, Texas, in 1967. Her first single, "Down on My Knees," was released in 1991 under her mother's maiden name of Ashton and sent her debut project, *Wakened by the Wind,* on to break sales records for the best-selling album by a new artist. Within a couple years she had reached No. 1 on the Christian charts numerous times, received a Dove Award, and been nominated for a Grammy Award, along with several other honors. She has recorded six albums and sold more than a million records of her own, as well as contributing to such prestigious projects as the Grammy-winning *Amazing Grace: A Country Salute to Gospel* and *Come Together: America Salutes the Beatles.* Her latest album, *Lost in Wonder,* a trio project with Michelle Tumes and Christine Denté, was released in 2005, and she has been working on a new solo project.

The Great . . . Beyond

Early in my career I had a mentor, someone who looked after the business side of things. But somewhere along the way, something happened. Even after all these years I'm still not sure when it occurred, but the bond of trust between us frayed. It wasn't pretty, but then again, no true test of character is.

They say business isn't personal, but when the tie between us was severed, I felt it; and when I experience an emotion that deeply, I can't help but voice it.

I know we don't see eye to eye

We've let angry hearts flare

And the bitter words fly

The common ground we used to share

Is harder to find but I believe that it's still there

What happened between us was basic human nature. Still, it's not easy to forgive. Letting the other guy off the hook, letting bygones go on by is easier said than done.

When I was a child and I did something naughty, Dad would dispense his discipline then immediately pray with me, making sure I was reminded of God's love, and his own. But for most of us, forgiveness requires forgetting, and that's difficult to do—especially if you're female. We tend to remember everything and file it away for future reference.

I couldn't forget. That disagreement day so long ago kept repeating in my head like an old vinyl record, scratched beyond repair. It played over and over in my mind. And with each skip back, my heart ached a little more.

I don't know if now is the time

To surrender the silence

Between your heart and mine

But the love that I've chosen

Cries out to be spoken

Leaving the heartache behind

In the heat of the moment too few of us recognize that split second of opportunity. We let the moment get the best of us, allowing the ties that should bond us, to bind us.

We're human; and the trappings of our humanity are what trip us up. We have a one-sided outlook, a limited perspective. And being mere mortals our own selfish sense of justice often blinds us to the obvious; that answer just past our logic . . . in the great beyond.

We must reach out beyond justice to mercy

Going more than halfway to forgive

It is the challenge each of us will face at least once in our lives; the effort to show mercy when we don't feel like doing so. Sure, the act of forgiveness itself is liberating. But getting to that place—and staying there—is the test. To pass that challenge we have to be willing to go a little further.

Our hearts forgive, but our minds don't forget. If we only go halfway, there will be occasions when we'd like to dredge it all up and throw it back in the offender's face. If we are not willing to take that extra step, we're just pretending to forget, and our wounds only pretend to mend. If poked and prodded the bruises will just become more inflamed.

However if we are willing to go more than halfway, we'll let go of that desire to throw it back in someone's face, and instead give it to God. And in turn, he will throw it into the sea of forgetfulness, to be dredged up no more. Then our forgiveness can become genuine, and though the bruises may linger, the touchy subject will no longer be tender.

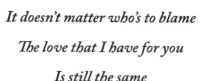

It doesn't matter who's to blame

The love that I have for you

Is still the same

The word *forgive* is amazing. If you break it down, it appears to mean, "before . . . give." *Before* it is deserved, *give* mercy. That's what God does for us every day; he withholds his judgment, and gives us grace before it is deserved. And it is never deserved.

A tender voice is calling me

To that place of compassion

Where hearts run pure and free

Where the hunger for vengeance

Gives way to repentance

Where love will teach us to see

On the cross Jesus prayed for the forgiveness of those who nailed him there: "for they know not what they do." Like the lyrics of a song, his words were brief and full of meaning. And his offer was made even before the deed was completed.

The forgiveness he provided that day was not just for the Romans and temple priests who conspired against him, but for every life lived before his coming, and every soul who had yet to be born—long before our first transgression.

His mercy was so genuine, his forgiveness so complete, that even though the wounds in his hands remained, the memory of the pain was no more. His forgiveness transformed the recollection of that horrible day from a course of ongoing irritation to the ultimate source of eternal inspiration.

And though his bruises still remain to this day, they are not tender to the touch. In fact, he welcomes anyone who is willing to take his nail-scarred hand.

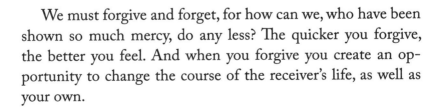

And though the distance seems so far

The love that used to hold our hearts

Longs to take us beyond justice to mercy

We must forgive and forget, for how can we, who have been shown so much mercy, do any less? The quicker you forgive, the better you feel. And when you forgive you create an opportunity to change the course of the receiver's life, as well as your own.

The wounds I received on that disagreement day so long ago were not pretty. But the scars that character test inflicted were mended when I reached beyond my own sense of justice.

Giving it to God, putting it in his hands, was like praying with Dad. And that's one memory I hope I never forget—that feeling of mercy beyond justice.

None of us deserves grace . . . and therein lies the definition.

⚶ Prayer ⚶

Help me to be ever mindful that I should judge not, lest I be judged. Let me never lose sight of the wonder that when I give, I will likewise be given. And remind me every day, seventy-seven times, that I should always be the first to go more than halfway to forgive.

But when the kindness and love of God our Savior appeared, he saved us, not because of righteous things we had done, but because of his mercy. He saved us through the washing of rebirth and renewal by the Holy Spirit, whom he poured out on us generously through Jesus Christ our Savior, so that, having been justified by his grace, we might become heirs having the hope of eternal life.

TITUS 3:4-7

Beyond Justice to Mercy

BY SUSAN ASHTON, BILLY SMILEY, AND PAULA CARPENTER

I know we don't see eye to eye
We've let angry hearts flare
And the bitter words fly
The common ground we used
   to share
Is harder to find but I believe that
   it's still there

I don't know if now is the time
To surrender the silence
Between your heart and mine
But the love that I've chosen
Cries out to be spoken
Leaving the heartache behind

We must reach out beyond justice
   to mercy
Going more than halfway to forgive
And though the distance seems
   so far
The love that used to hold our hearts
Longs to take us beyond justice
   to mercy

It doesn't matter who's to blame
The love that I have for you
Is still the same
A tender voice is calling me
To that place of compassion
Where hearts run pure and free
Where the hunger for vengeance
Gives way to repentance
Where love will teach us to see

Matthew
West

Matthew West grew up as a pastor's kid in suburban Chicago. After high school graduation, his dad gave him a guitar, which started Matthew on the road to becoming an independent artist. Once out of college he traveled the country, performing at schools and coffeehouses and earning recognition from the National Association of Campus Activities. He later moved to Nashville and became the first Christian artist signed to the Universal South record label.

His first single on his 2003 debut album, *Happy*, held the No. 1 spot on R&R's Christian Adult Contemporary chart for a record-breaking nine weeks and was named Christian Song of the Year by ASCAP. His album entitled *History* was released in the summer of 2005. He has received several nominations for GMA Music Awards, including two for Song of the Year for 2006. West has also had his songs recorded by many of the top names in Christian music and has written for a column in *CCM Magazine.*

When not on the road, Matthew lives outside Nashville with his wife, Emily, and their pug, Earl "The Girl." Their baby girl, Luella Jane, was welcomed by the family in January of 2006.

Window of Opportunity

Two weeks . . . fourteen days. As I walked through the yard to my house, the words bounced around in my head like the chorus of a catchy tune. I was almost giddy. I felt like a kid counting down the final days to Christmas, but it was the last week of July. And the gift I was expecting wasn't a toy train set, but the vehicle that would put my career on the fast track.

Just two more weeks. The notion put a spring in my step as I paced off the final few feet to my front door. The dream I had watched others attain, the goal I had worked so hard to achieve was now, finally, within my reach.

Without breaking my stride I took hold of the doorknob, turned and pushed. All of my anticipation, all the inertia of my forward thinking carried me across the threshold. Then—*BLAM!* I collided with an unexpected, bone-jarring barricade. The door was locked.

I jiggled the knob and leaned into it. Nothing. My fingers dove into every pocket I had. No keys. As my hands searched, my mind started its own inventory. This wasn't my first run-in with this door. Nor was it the first time I had to consider improvising another way in.

Growing up as a pastor's kid just outside of Chicago, my path was often blocked by well-meaning parishioners who pinched my adolescent cheeks and gushed, "You're gonna grow up to be a preacher, just like your dad, right?" Never knowing how to tactfully answer, I'd smile through my red, stinging cheeks and scan the sanctuary for the nearest exit.

Choosing a vocation, especially the door Dad had walked through, gave me pause; his selfless, 24-hour-a-day job had always required more courage and strength than I could ever muster. And though my parents' faith was an inspiration, I chose another way and set my teenage sights on a career far less strenuous—sports.

All through high school I kept one eye on the ball and the other searching the grandstands for that football or baseball scout who would offer me a scholarship—that door to the big leagues. But the elusive doorman never showed. And by the time senior year rolled around, I realized that I was going to have to improvise yet another way.

So with the sports door shut as tight as my front door, I reluctantly laid down my ball glove, picked up my hobby—my guitar—and began to play. It took a while, but eventually I worked my way up to touring the college circuit and writing songs for other artists. That's when the elusive doorman finally showed up—not on the sidelines of some ball field, but in the audience of a record label showcase.

Now everything was going my way. I was dating an amazing girl, Emily, and I was two weeks away from crossing the threshold of a new musical career. There was just one glitch. I couldn't get past my own front door.

The last time I locked myself out I discovered an alternate route, a window of opportunity. So doing my best Spider-man, I once more scaled the side of the house and began my encore acrobatic performance. But this time the handle of the old frame window didn't want to cooperate. Staying in one position for a long time tends to make some windows a real "pane." So I marshalled my strongest arm, pounding the frame with my left hand in a series of upward blows. Nothing.

I was about to sign a record deal that would change my life; I was on the verge of my biggest break! Surely, after improvising all of these alternate routes, I was capable of breaking into my own house through a window! So I pounded harder . . . and the glass exploded.

All of my frustration and impatience carried my arm through the frame and *BLAM!* My arm collided with a shower of skin-dicing shards. In a strange, surreal slow motion, I watched as a large wedge of glass sliced through the main artery of my strongest arm. Instantly everything was red. I had never seen so much blood.

Trying not to panic, I applied pressure with my right hand. But it didn't help. I started to run, screaming at the top of my lungs. "Help! Somebody! Help!" But in less than two minutes all of my strength was gone, drained out of me like air escaping from a punctured balloon. And I crumpled in my neighbor's front yard, wanting nothing more than to sleep.

Two weeks . . . just two more weeks. I could feel the dream I had worked so hard to achieve slipping away as fast as my blood spilled into the grass. The hand that would have signed my record contract could no longer move. This time there was no improvising another way. I was helpless.

❧

It's out of my hands

It's out of my reach

It's over my head

And it's out of my league

❧

As best as I could, I kept calling for help. But the bright July sun was getting dimmer with each blood-draining moment. Soon, all I could feel was a hint of the warm summer wind on my blue, numbing cheeks.

After what seemed forever, my delirium conjured two men wearing construction overalls, standing over me. My ears heard their fast, frantic words, but in my haze it was gibberish. One was talking on his cell phone, the other was tying his bandana around my arm. For some span of time they poured water over my face to keep me conscious, and continued their rapid back and forth gibberish. Finally, a single word they kept repeating over and over seemed familiar; it was the Spanish pronunciation of Jesus. My Hispanic rescuers were praying . . . and so was I.

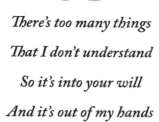

There's too many things

That I don't understand

So it's into your will

And it's out of my hands

When I came to, five days later, I was in a hospital bed surrounded by people. The first face I saw was Emily's. The moment she heard the news, she'd left her desk at the record company and had rarely left my side since my arrival by ambulance. The surgeons, likewise hovering over me, wouldn't let me look at my arm. But the expression on Mom and Dad's faces told me more than I wanted to know.

The glass had lacerated one of the two main arteries in my arm, coming within a centimeter of destroying the main nerves necessary for movement. Considering the damage, the doctors thought it best to tie the vein off and reroute its blood flow to the secondary artery. The procedure would have been just the ticket had the tie-off remained tied. But somehow the doctor's efforts had unraveled.

In short, it would take a year before the extent of the damage could be realized. And there was a high probability that my strongest arm would never be strong again. *Two weeks*. It might as well have been two centuries.

There you go changing my plans again

There you go shifting my sands again

For reasons I don't understand again

Lately I don't have a clue

What was I going to do? It takes two hands to play a guitar. If I can't play, what about Emily? Our plans? Our future? Had all my perspiration and self-motivation propelled me into a hospital bed? Did I have nothing else to look forward to but months of physical therapy?

The deadline for my contract passed without fanfare. And weeks later I was still far from well. The surgeons had rerouted the blood in my arm. But redirecting my thought patterns, my path to reason, was up to me. It was a task I had not auditioned for nor ever aspired to. I was standing at another locked door. I jiggled the knob and leaned into it. Nothing. And I couldn't find the key.

Playing the guitar was easy. Writing lyrics for a living was a breeze. But from my bed that dream vocation now seemed not only physically improbable, but mentally and emotionally impossible. In my mind I began to honestly examine the prospects of other occupations. At that moment, even Dad's job seemed easier.

Being a pastor, a 24/7 shepherd to many parishioners, had always seemed such a daunting task. But he handled it with confidence and ease. He knew his job and did it well. Even those construction workers who came to my rescue, they knew what to do. They called 911, wrapped up my arm, and kept me awake with water. Why were their difficult tasks so much easier than mine? What could a Chicago pastor and a couple of Nashville construction workers possibly have in common?

As my mind raced, it hit me—they never stopped repeating the name of Jesus.

It was like colliding with a bone-jarring barricade that just gave way. All of my anticipation and forward thinking had been spent trying to cross the threshold of my dreams—without paying proper attention to the door.

Just when I start liking what I see

There you go changing my scenery

I never know where you're taking me

But I'm trying just to follow you

Instead of improvising another way, I realized that I needed to be more aware of the (only) Way. Jesus, the Son of God, was the one who put me on my path. My parents had taught me well. It's just that sometimes, we get so busy with our dreams, we need reminding that his way is always better. And on occasion, learning that lesson may require a few locked doors, and a window of opportunity shattering, in slow motion.

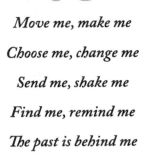

Move me, make me

Choose me, change me

Send me, shake me

Find me, remind me

The past is behind me

With the optimism of a Spider-man wannabe, I crossed the room and forced myself to sit down at a piano. It wasn't my instrument of choice, but it did allow me the option of using one hand. Struggling, I started plucking out chords, one note at a time. And as I began to scribble down some words, I realized that the insights I was composing with my weak hand could never have been written with the strong.

There you go healing these scars again

Showing me right where you are again

I'm helpless, and that's where I start again

I'm giving it all up to you

They say that all new artists spend their lives writing that first CD. But all those tunes paled in comparison to the words and music I discovered while gazing through my broken window of opportunity. Even my record label heard the difference. And they gave me the time to mend, restring my guitar, rethink my first album, and get married.

When you put your future in God's hands, it's amazing what you can do; even with a weak arm.

⸕ Prayer ⸕

Let me dream big, but never so large that I overlook your plans. And help me to always see the blockades in my path for what they are—reminders to stop and look for you.

> I am the door: by me if any man enter in, he shall be saved, and shall go in and out, and find pasture.
>
> JOHN 10:9 *(KJV)*

Out of My Hands

⸖ BY MATTHEW WEST AND SAM MIZELL ⸖

There you go changing my
  plans again
There you go shifting my
    sands again
For reasons I don't understand again
Lately I don't have a clue

Just when I start liking what I see
There you go changing my scenery
I never know where you're
    taking me
But I'm trying just to follow you

Chorus:
It's out of my hands
It's out of my reach
It's over my head
And it's out of my league
There's too many things
That I don't understand
So it's into your will
And it's out of my hands

There you go healing these
    scars again
Showing me right where you
    are again
I'm helpless, and that's where I
    start again
I'm giving it all up to you

Repeat Chorus

Bridge:
Move me, make me
Choose me, change me
Send me, shake me
Find me, remind me
The past is behind me

Take it all away
Take it all from me, I pray

Repeat Chorus

Margaret Becker

Through a singing/songwriting career of twenty years, Margaret Becker has accumulated fourteen albums (including her latest, the Psalms-based *Faithfully Yours*), four Dove Awards, four Grammy nominations, and twenty No. 1 radio hits. She's been named Songwriter of the Year by *American Songwriter* magazine, an honor she's also received seven times from the performance rights organization SESAC. She has written numerous articles and has authored four books—*With New Eyes* (Harvest House), *Growing Up Together* (Harvest House), *Braving the Elements* (RandomHouse/Waterbrook Press), and her latest title, *Coming Up for Air* (Navpress).

Margaret is dedicated to encouraging people to reach their creative potential and engage in deeper Christian faith and service. This passion informs her work as a writer, speaker, guest lecturer, mentor, and record producer. She launched her own music publishing company, Modernm, in 2003, and in that same year received from the Convocation of Episcopal Churches in Europe the Lumiére du Monde Award, honoring her global advocacy work.

Since 1993, she has been a partner with and spokesperson for World Vision, the Seattle-based global relief agency, and has recently established the Orange Fund, which collects and distributes resources to the most needy areas in the African AIDS crisis.

MARGARET BECKER

Living in the Moment

There is an instant just before dawn when it is neither light nor dark. Then . . . wait for it . . . a sudden explosion of color lights up the sky—wispy blues, yellows, shades of orange and red. They appear out of nowhere, as if an unseen painter has swirled his brush across the horizon. The hues constantly move, spilling into each other, forming new palettes, new shapes among the meandering clouds. Then, after mere moments, the show is over and the day begins.

Sitting on an empty beach, watching this cosmic display of performance art, I felt that God was putting on a light show for an audience of one. It was just me, the crashing waves, and the cool November wind. Some may think that going to Florida in the fall is the right place at the wrong time. But my reasons for being on that beach had nothing to with the location or the season. It had everything to do with where I stood with God, and the amount of time we spent together. Because he is everywhere, I could've been anywhere.

If we were each granted a ride on the space shuttle, and were able to look directly down onto our personal spot on the planet, it would appear from that lofty height that each of us was living at the center of the globe. God shaped this world in such a way that, no matter where we are, we occupy the center of his circle. Each of us has his undivided attention.

But sadly, we rarely give him the same consideration. We just don't seem to have enough hours in the day. And that was my problem.

Being a songwriter, I'm an observer of the world. But when it came to my own globe, it had become a spinning blur of distractions. Recording, performing, traveling—it seemed somehow my living had got in the way of my life. Before I arrived on that beach, I felt myself being pulled in every direction. I was dwelling on the past, dreaming about the future, always rushing to meet the next deadline—trying to outrun the sun and avoid the dark. Slowing down was not an option. And spending time with the one who had created time—well, he wasn't even a pencilled scribble in my day planner.

When I observed the glaring omission of him from my life, I realized my problem was a matter of time. So I forced my spinning world to a grinding halt. I stepped off, stopped the clock, and decided to live in the moment.

Choosing a place that was out of the way, I cleared off my calendar and picked my spot in the sand. There, looking at the ocean, I blocked out all distractions, opened up my senses to the sights and sounds around me, and focused my attention on the creator of it all . . .

I think I heard your voice floating on the evening wind

And you near again in the touch of a friend

This is life as it should be

This is life complete

Cracking the surface of every breath

And finding you there in the center of it

Knowing that I occupied the center of God's circle, I tried to encircle myself with him. I gave the creator my undivided attention, from sunrise to sunrise.

Since the beginning of creation, God's light show has had two performances a day, morning and evening. Yet too few of us take the time to notice. I wanted to drink it all in—savor every color, every texture, every pattern.

As I sat with my toes in the sand and listened to the roar of the ocean, I gazed out at the colorful curtain of light and marveled. Just outside the atmosphere, just backstage of this performance, there was an intricate dance of gravity, planets, and stars—all moving at his command—making this magnificent piece of art possible, just for me.

In the beauty of the morning, in the rhythm of the rain

In the symphony of laughter as it plays across the face

In the colors of creation painting sunsets in the fall

I want to feel it all

At dusk there's an instant when it is neither light nor dark. Then . . . wait for it . . . the orange-yellow sun sinks below the horizon, and evening comes. Some think that the darkness is the worst of times, but it's not so. In whatever state you find yourself, it is up to you to make it a disaster or a delight.

I was living in the moment, surrounded by God, and in the center of his circle the darkness was far from a portent of doom. Have you ever noticed the order of the original sunrise and sunset? "And God said, 'Let there be light,' . . . God called the light 'day,' and the darkness he called 'night.' And there was evening, and there was morning—the first day" (Genesis 1:3-5).

The evening, the night, came first! In the Genesis account of creation, a day does not start with the first rays of the eastern sun. As it was in the beginning, every new day dawns in the dark.

On creation's first morning, God gave us an example of how he works behind the scenes. He showed us that even when things appear dark—when it seems we are out of options, out of time, beyond hope—he is beyond the horizon, moving the universe around, just for us. And all it takes to notice this piece of performance art is to stop and live in the moment.

Joshua did.

Like me, the Old Testament warrior had a problem with scheduling. He had a battle to win and darkness was falling. But Joshua did not accept the notion of looming disaster. Instead he opted for delight. Hearing the soldier's prayer, God intervened and left the lights on, actually stopping the sun in the sky (Joshua 10:12-14).

King Hezekiah lived in the moment too. He had no choice; every minute that passed brought him closer to death. The king was sick, wasting away, when Isaiah the prophet stopped by to tell him the obvious: "You will die, and not live." Hezekiah was teetering on the brink of darkness. But even though it seemed he was beyond hope, he called to the one beyond the horizon.

Hearing the king's petition, God ordered Isaiah back to the king's deathbed. As a sign of the creator's intervention, the prophet asked the king which way the shadow on the stairway should move. The sick man answered, "Backwards." The shadow retreated, extra sunlight was added to the day, and years were added to the king's life (2 Kings 20:1-11). Hezekiah pushed back the dark and chose delight, and in turn God pushed back the shadows.

That's living in the moment—feeling it all.

What is life if not to see your Spirit passing by?

And what is love if not to leave the imprint of your touch?

I think I see it

While most people use their vacation to sleep in and piddle around, I felt reenergized. So much so that I challenged myself to rise early enough every morning to witness the dawn—to experience God's incredible performance art.

Every day he turns on the light and encourages us to likewise rise and shine. Life is not a rehearsal, just ask Hezekiah. When the sun rises each morning so does the curtain.

Been living so close to the skin, trying to feel everything

Been digging down so deep, looking for eternal things

So I prayed a prayer to be wise

I prayed a prayer to see it with your eyes

For ears to hear and a heart to seek

And the gift to find all the colors you leave

Sitting on that beach, enjoying the wispy blues and the shades of orange and red, I got the swirling patterns of my living and my life sorted out. I set things straight and realized that I never want my past or my future to get in the way of my present. All we are truly given is now—*this* moment.

Every day under the sun is a once-in-a-lifetime opportunity to move; to spill our life experiences into each other; to form new palettes, new alliances; to connect with those meandering souls who never have enough time. Every day is another chance to live in the moment.

Between the light and the dark there is an instant of choice. Live it. Feel it all. Make time for God. He moved around the universe, pushed back the shadows and created time for you.

⫸ PRAYER ⫷

Never let my calendar get in the way of our time together. And when the fears of the night have me questioning tomorrow, let me walk with you, the creator of the light, and remember that as sure as the sun rises in the east, my darkest moments are just the dawning of a brand new day.

> "And God said, 'Let there be light.'"
>
> GENESIS 1:3

Feel It All

WORDS AND MUSIC BY MARGARET BECKER AND ROBBIE NEVILL

I think I heard your voice floating
  on the evening wind
And you near again in the touch
  of a friend
This is life as it should be
  this is life complete
Cracking the surface of every breath
And finding you there in the
    center of it

In the beauty of the morning
  in the rhythm of the rain
In the symphony of laughter as it
  plays across the face
In the colors of creation painting
  sunsets in the fall
I want to feel it all

Been living so close to the skin,
  trying to feel everything
Been digging down so deep, looking
  for eternal things
So I prayed a prayer to be wise,
  I prayed a prayer to see it
  with your eyes
For ears to hear and a heart to seek
And the gift to find all the colors
  you leave

In the beauty of the morning,
  in the rhythm of the rain
In the symphony of laughter as it
  plays across the face
In the colors of creation painting
  sunsets in the fall
I want to feel it all

What is life if not to see your Spirit
  passing by?
And what is love if not to leave the
  imprint of your touch?
I think I see it

In the beauty of the morning,
  in the rhythm of the rain
In the symphony of laughter as it
  plays across the face
In the colors of creation painting
  sunsets in the fall
I want to feel it all

In the fury of the ocean on a stormy
  winter's day
In the choir of the angels as they
  dance upon the waves
In the colors of creation painting
  sunsets in the fall
I want to feel it all

Russ
Taff

Russ Taff was born in 1953, the fourth of five sons, to a Pentecostal preacher father and a gospel music-loving mother. He began his career after moving to Arkansas in his teens, where he formed a band called Sounds of Joy that eventually opened for the legendary Imperials. Two years after this opening, Russ joined the Imperials as lead vocalist. Four and a half years later, he decided to pursue a solo career in which he explored his eclectic musical tastes, ranging from rock to big band to southern gospel.

Since 1991 Russ has appeared as a regular artist in the Gaither Homecoming concerts. In 2001 he joined the Gaither Vocal Band as a baritone, but about three years later decided to return to his place as a solo artist on tour.

Over the course of his career, his distinctive style has earned him five Grammy Awards and nine Dove Awards. Russ has often collaborated on his albums with his wife, Tori, whom he has described as his "favorite lyricist."

Preconceived Notions

It was 4 AM. I was tired and frustrated. I needed another song for my first solo album, but the pen in my hand wouldn't move. The page was blank, intimidating. The only lines my mind could conjure were the not-so-invisible boundaries that had divided my world.

I was twenty-two. My musical career was taking off. Tori and I had just married and were mostly on the road, performing solo concerts and touring with the Imperials. For a while traveling, singing, and spreading the good news was everything we dreamed it could be. But with every state line we ventured across, we discovered another more tangible divide.

It was the 1980s, a time when a memorable TV commercial showed a hillside covered with people holding hands and swaying to the words, "I'd like to teach the world to sing, in perfect harmony." The notion was appealing, inclusive. That is, to everyone but the Christians of the day. Back then, holding hands and harmonizing with anyone—especially someone who belonged to another denomination—was just not done. In those days it was practically considered blasphemy if a Pentecostal went to a Baptist concert, or vice versa.

While we were on the road singing "Listen to the trumpet of Jesus," some of our fellow Christians were obsessing over the "different sound." On national television, a prominent evangelist was spending valuable airtime blacklisting artists like me, the Imperials, and others, because we did not conform to his preconceived notion of gospel music.

And while we were trying to "march to the drumbeat of God Almighty," many of our brothers and sisters were wandering around preoccupied with hair length and clothing styles. Even to a kid in his twenties the situation was immature and divisive. As I sat in our small west Nashville apartment in the middle of the night, the only lines my mind could focus on were the scrimmage lines of separation. All I could envision were images of high walls—immovable roadblocks against which my own gullible illusions were shattered. I wanted to write a song about the love of God, yet all I could think about was the prejudice of man. And it was in the middle of this frustration that my pen finally began to move.

Sometimes it's hard for me to understand

Why we pull away from each other so easily

Even though we're all walkin' the same road

Yet we build dividing walls between

Our brothers and ourselves

It seemed obvious to me that our superficial differences were petty and irrelevant. And if our contrasts have no effect on the population of Heaven, it just doesn't matter.

~

I don't care what label you may wear

If you believe in Jesus you belong with me

The bond we share is all I care to see

We can change this world forever

If you'll join with me, join and sing

~

Music is amazing. In the short time it took to record these lyrics and mass-distribute the album, I discovered that I wasn't alone. That vinyl disk became a musical magnifying glass, exploring not only the times and my best hopes, but also the sentiment of the larger Christian community.

Immediately folks such as Billy Graham latched on to its musical message, and he started using the song as an anthem in his crusades. Then Bill and Gloria Gaither reprised the song as an invitation to "come home" and join their ever-growing family of friends.

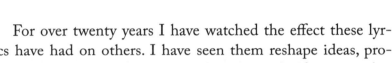

You're my brother, you're my sister

So take me by the hand

Together we will work until he comes

There's no foe that can defeat us

When we're walkin' side by side

As long as there is love

We will stand

For over twenty years I have watched the effect these lyrics have had on others. I have seen them reshape ideas, promote dialogue, and help banish the preconceived notions that have surrounded me. Of course, I'm pleased that this wave of examination was initiated by my song, but I'm not surprised. The human desire for improvement is far from a novel notion.

For me, self-exploration is an ongoing exercise, a journey of improvement that never ends. Still, facing my self is never easy—in fact it is physically impossible. The only person you have the power to change is the one person you cannot see bodily—yourself. Athletes must resort to the instant replay to improve their game. Actors depend on the critique of the director and the audience for their insight. In every walk of life, self-improvement requires the involvement of someone outside yourself, holding that magnifying glass.

When I penned those words that dark, frustrating night, *I* was the outsider, commenting on a society that was so caught up in its prejudices that people couldn't see their own actions. And when that magnifying glass was turned my way, I too was so caught up in the moment that both my prejudice and the outsider startled me.

On that revealing day, I was ironically in the middle of my latest self-improvement kick—walking. Whether I was home in Nashville with Tori and our girls, Charlotte and Maddie Rose, or on the road doing a string of concerts, I had made it a priority to carve out a portion of every day for a vigorous, heart-pumping hike. It was during one of these strolls down a busy San Jose street that I discovered something about myself I never imagined.

It was around noon, and the California sun shone down on a city sidewalk filled with hungry pedestrians, all trying to make the most of their lunch break. Meandering through this moving maze, I briskly stepped off the curb to cross the street. From the opposite corner a woman approached. At first she was just another face in the crowd, that is, until we were about to pass on the crosswalk.

"You be careful down here."

Her unexpected words took me off guard and broke my concentration. My eyes darted in her direction. That's when I noticed she was dirty, disheveled, and pushing a grocery cart filled with items salvaged from the garbage. In that instant I came to the all-inclusive conclusion: *homeless*.

Instinctively reaching into my pocket, I pulled out three dollar bills and put them in her hand. I smiled and walked on, subconsciously relieved. *There, I've dealt with you.*

I had only taken a few steps when a voice inside me whispered, *Go back. Talk to her.* The words were as clear and as unexpected as the woman's greeting. And my response was just as sharp. *No! She's filthy, and very likely a loon!* But my walking shoes turned of their own accord and I soon found myself navigating my way back through the crowd.

My eyes scanned for the grocery cart. I was sure that the woman and my three dollars were headed for the nearest liquor store. But through the forest of bobbing heads, I spotted her opening the door to a coffee shop.

By the time I entered the establishment, she was sitting at a table with her only companions—her cart and her just-purchased lunch of an apple and coffee.

Hesitantly I approached her. "Excuse me. Can I talk to you?"

She looked up from her steaming cup of java a little befuddled.

"I'm the guy who just gave you three dollars."

A sudden look of recognition crossed her worn face. "Please," she smiled, "have a seat."

After a few awkward moments, our conversation slowly took on the rhythm of a good walk. Her name was Portia, and the heartbreaking story of her sixty years was a marathon tale of hard luck and love lost. Looking into her dark sunken eyes, I realized that the labels I had sung against so adamantly I had placed on her instantly. And peeling away those preconceived notions, I could see that this wandering, lonely outsider had once been pretty.

The California sun and that self-examining magnifying glass started working on me, burning a hole in my pride. And it didn't take long before the wall I had built between my sister and myself began to melt.

"How would you like a real, hot meal?" I asked. Her blue eyes lit up.

Portia and I ended up spending the rest of the day together, walking and talking. As the sun started down, I escorted her and her cart back to the arena where I was booked that night. Somewhere along the way she took my arm and started singing an old Everly Brothers song from her youth. And swaying to the tune, I harmonized.

Backstage in the arena's greenroom, Portia was stunned by the sight of tables upon tables of food. Standing back, I got a kick out of watching the other artists on the marquee stop by her piled-high plate to chat. Each one treated this outsider with the kindness and respect we all deserve from each other. And it was then that I fully recognized my own prejudice.

Our differences should be icebreakers, not wall-makers. If it doesn't affect the population of Heaven, it just doesn't matter. That day I realized that there is only one preconceived notion we should entertain.

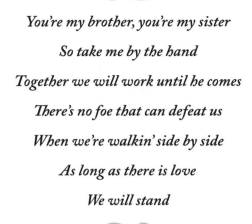

You're my brother, you're my sister

So take me by the hand

Together we will work until he comes

There's no foe that can defeat us

When we're walkin' side by side

As long as there is love

We will stand

There will come a time when our long, frustrating night as outsiders will finally be over. On that bright day I'll see Portia again. All of my personal baggage will be gone and so will her cart. Together, we will walk side by side. I'll take her by the hand and . . . harmonize.

⟨ Prayer ⟩

No more labels. Let me always look beyond the facade and see your face. And remind me every day that if our disagreements do not affect the population of Heaven, they just don't matter.

> You hypocrite, first take the plank out of your own eye, and then you will see clearly to remove the speck from your brother's eye.

MATTHEW 7:5

We Will Stand

♪ WORDS BY RUSS AND TORI TAFF ♪
MUSIC BY JAMES HOLLIHAN

Sometimes it's hard for me to
understand
Why we pull away from each other
so easily
Even though we're all walkin' the
same road
Yet we build dividing walls between
Our brothers and ourselves

I don't care what label you may wear
If you believe in Jesus you belong
with me
The bond we share is all I care to see
We can change this world forever
If you'll join with me, join and sing

Chorus:
You're my brother, you're my sister
So take me by the hand
Together we will work until he comes
There's no foe that can defeat us
When we're walkin' side by side
As long as there is love
We will stand

The day will come when we'll
be as one
And with a mighty voice
Together we will proclaim
Jesus Christ is King
It will echo through the earth
It will shake the nations
And the world will see . . .

Repeat Chorus

Cindy Morgan

Cindy Morgan has come a long way since her humble childhood in Red Hill, Tennessee. Moving near Nashville after high school, Cindy took on odd jobs until she landed a part in a daily show at Dollywood. An audition tape she made for *Star Search* ended up at Word Records, where her singing/songwriting career took off. Her 1992 debut resulted in three No. 1 singles, and the following year she won the Dove Award for New Artist of the Year.

Over the years Cindy has accumulated seven albums, twelve No. 1 radio hits, and six Dove Awards. She has written songs for such award-winning artists as Michael W. Smith, Michelle Tumes, Sandi Patty, BeBe Winans, Rachael Lampa, Jaci Velasquez, and many others. She has also authored a book, *Barefoot on Barbed Wire* (Harvest House, 2001). Her album entitled *Postcards* was released in 2006. Five years in the making, the album marks a return to performing her own songs.

Cindy and her family—author husband, Sigmund Brouwer, and their two daughters—split their time between their homes in Canada and Nashville.

Moving Day

Memories—they can make us or break us. Those lingering, often languishing images from the past can compel us to cry or propel us to fly. My memories did both.

I was raised in a log cabin in a holler tucked deep in the hills of eastern Tennessee. It was a hard life and my only means of escape was inward; for as far back as I can remember I've sustained myself with lyrical prayers and melodies of my own making.

Over the years as my circumstances got harder, my spiritual life grew deeper and composing came more easily. Eventually, that ability to get away through music provided me with just the ticket necessary to escape the hills—and I took it. On that moving day, I packed my bags in a blur and left, never wanting to look back.

My journey eventually led me to Nashville, to Word Records, and to a musical career that my cabin days had helped to fashion, but could never have imagined. The faith I had clung to as a little girl inside that crowded house I was now singing about on spacious concert stages. The painful human conditions I experienced in that isolated holler I now voiced in harmony to thousands of fans. For years my life was writing, recording, and the road; repeatedly singing about the insights I first discovered during a time I just wanted to forget.

But the further we move to distance ourselves from the things we don't want to face, the closer they come, and the sooner they reappear. Why? We can retreat only so far in one direction—the world is round.

When the past finally materialized again on my horizon, I was working on the *Elementary* album, back in Tennessee. Suddenly, I found myself staring out at the distant hazy mountains that surrounded my childhood home. Although my family no longer lived there, something compelled me forward. It was the one place I didn't want to go. Still, like a moth to a flame, I was drawn ever closer.

A young tennis coach answered the door. After explaining that I had once lived where he now hangs his racket and beer posters, he invited me across the threshold, into the past.

Every creak in the floor, every splinter in the wall conjured a memory. In these rooms my father, mother, sisters, and brothers went about the daily struggles of living. In these rooms, watching their lives, my life was shaped. Although I was the youngest, with no idea what life was all about, somehow I knew that the way things were, were not the way they should be. And when the echo of loud voices and images of my mother's anguish began to resurface, I ended my tour and journeyed back down the road of denial.

Maybe it was because I was married now and my husband and I were in the middle of packing to move to a bigger place, but I couldn't shake those rekindled memories of my family and my visit to the cabin. Even though our moving day was approaching and the future before us was bright, I found myself stuck in the past, reliving the emotions I felt back in those rooms.

Haunted by those distant mountain memories, I had to do something. So I descended into our cluttered basement, through a maze of half-packed boxes, and found my way to my time-tested instrument of escape, my piano. As I sat at the keyboard, I just let go. The chords were muffled by the surrounding cardboard boxes, but I played on, unloading baggage that had remained sealed since my first moving day, years before.

∾

In these rooms dark and bare

I recall when life was living here

How we sang and how we cried

A little of us lived here

A little of us died

Mama she knew how to sing

But her eyes were always sad and wondering

∾

Sitting there, I relived my mother's struggle. She never had the chance to be a little girl. Her father left her mother with six children during the depths of the depression. Mom, being the oldest of the brood, was forced to become a parent before she was even a teenager. And like my own childhood memories, Mom's past followed her too.

You see her daddy drank

And he ran around

He ran away with all her dreams

And she looked just like an angel

With broken wings

My sister she was a wild little thing

With a heart made of gold

But if you didn't look deep inside her

You might never know

My sister, the oldest girl, inherited all of my mother's baggage. Like Mom, she had to help care for her younger siblings. Dad, though he worked hard, always came home with his sleeves rolled up, ready to pitch in. He did all he could. But my sister's struggles were troubles that not even a father's help could repair.

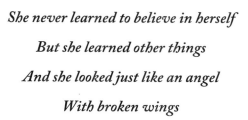

She never learned to believe in herself

But she learned other things

And she looked just like an angel

With broken wings

My ability to get away through music had helped me to escape the hills. My gift had been my ticket out. But there, in my box-cluttered basement, I realized that my ticket was a round-trip.

I never liked my mama's daddy

For more reasons than I can share

My mama held him as he died

And I'm ashamed to say I never cried or cared

Singing out loud what I had never allowed myself to think lifted the heavy bags off my shoulders and helped me to see things more clearly. My mother's father never examined his life. He never questioned his selfishness, nor cared how his actions affected others. He never faced himself.

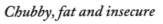

Chubby, fat and insecure

Two crooked teeth

And clothes from a thrift store

My mother's father lived his life in denial. But my mother didn't make the same mistake. Although Grandfather tried to distance himself from everything, including facing his own death, Mom held him in her arms, gazed at him wide-eyed, and made sure that her forgiving smile was the last thing he saw.

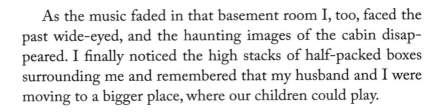

In these rooms

Dark and bare

What once seemed

So confusing

Seems crystal clear

As the music faded in that basement room I, too, faced the past wide-eyed, and the haunting images of the cabin disappeared. I finally noticed the high stacks of half-packed boxes surrounding me and remembered that my husband and I were moving to a bigger place, where our children could play.

They say that angels have wings because they take things lightly. I guess it's because they don't have any baggage. At that moment I felt like an angel, ready for moving day.

❧ PRAYER ☙

Help me to be aware of the rooms I live in, the words I speak, the deeds I do. Let me always be mindful of how my decisions affect others. Let me face every problem head-on, even if the problem is me.

> "Then you will know the truth, and the truth will set you free."
>
> JOHN 8:32

In These Rooms

WORDS AND MUSIC BY CINDY MORGAN

In these rooms dark and bare
I recall when life was living here
How we sang and how we cried
A little of us lived here
A little of us died
Mama she knew how to sing
But her eyes were always sad and
    wondering
You see her daddy drank
And he ran around
He ran away with all her dreams
And she looked just like an angel
With broken wings

My sister she was a wild little thing
With a heart made of gold
But if you didn't look deep
    inside her
You might never know
She never learned to believe in herself
But she learned other things
And she looked just like an angel
With broken wings

Chorus:
Broken angel
You can learn how to fly
Let the wind carry you
Far deep and wide
Beautiful angel
Well, it's OK to cry
'Cause your tears will bloom
Someday on the other side

I never liked my mama's daddy
For more reasons than I can share
My mama held him as he died
And I'm ashamed to say I never
    cried or cared
Chubby, fat and insecure
Two crooked teeth
And clothes from a thrift store
Well I never quite fit in
I guess that's why I'm singing

Repeat Chorus

In these rooms
Dark and bare
What once seemed
So confusing
Seems crystal clear
If I were to look back into you
The way you've looked down to me
I bet you'd look just like an angel
I bet you'd look a whole lot like
    me, yeah
I bet you'd look just like an angel
Oh, with broken wings

Repeat Chorus

Yeah, your tears will bloom someday
On the other side

Anthony Burger

One of gospel music's premier musicians, Anthony Burger delighted audiences worldwide for more than twenty-five years. He offered inspired music together with an inspiring testimony of God's healing. After a childhood accident resulting in severe burns, doctors said Anthony would never move his hands again. But Anthony thanked God every day that "the doctors were wrong, and that I stayed with it and play for him."

It was God's healing grace, combined with his mother's encouragement, that brought him at the age of five to be accepted as the youngest student ever at Chattanooga's Cadek Conservatory. Anthony later combined years of classical piano training, his natural gifts, and broad musical experiences in a career that led him to achieve numerous awards and performances at a wide variety of settings such as the White House, the Billy Graham Crusades, the Gaither Homecoming Tours, Broadway, Carnegie Hall, and TNN's Prime Time Country television program.

Though an average of 200 concerts a year kept him busy, he was a dedicated family man and loved spending time with his wife, Luanne, and his children A.J., Austin, and Lori.

In February of 2006, Anthony died suddenly at the age of 44 in the middle of doing what he loved, playing the piano. On being asked once what had kept him going after so many years and so many performances, Anthony had answered, "I am a simple man with a majestic instrument and the power of God behind me." That's the life he lived, and the legacy that lives on in the hearts of his family, friends, and fans.

Being Instrumental

Two hands descend on eighty-eight keys. The moment of contact is explosive, magical. When mortal skin collides with a keyboard of ivory, it triggers vibrations in the surrounding air, and the sound produced can be either a big bang or a melodic chord.

Between blaring chaos and beautiful composition there is a fine line. I know; I stumbled across it.

For over three decades my fingers have enjoyed the delight of colliding with a piano's eighty-eight keys. The music produced by that contact has rattled the rafters of Carnegie Hall, vibrated the chandeliers of the White House, and allowed me to travel the world. But this whirlwind life of music and travel might never have happened; my hands might never have known this level of skill on a keyboard if my feet had not first fumbled across a floorboard.

I'm not clumsy, just curious. As early as eight months old, I was aware of the world around me and was already exploring it with the help of a walker—basically a diaper on wheels. Once I discovered the concept of putting one foot in front of another, my little transporter allowed me to go just about anywhere.

I was able to follow the smells of my mother's cooking into a large place called the kitchen, and negotiate my way around a menagerie of scattered instruments from my folks' successful music store.

My vehicle even permitted me to approach the hallway leading to the uncharted lairs of my older siblings' bedrooms. The narrow passage to that forbidden territory was a virtual obstacle course; before me lay a long, slippery stretch of hardwood interrupted midway by a dark pit covered with a metal grate. Being too young to comprehend caution and too curious to stay put, I eventually took an extra step, rolling my wheeled transporter onto the cold wood floor.

Coasting down the corridor was a giddy experience, but the journey abruptly ended at the edge of the grate. One of the wheels of my walker got caught in the metal frame and the momentum toppled me over—onto the floor vent of the furnace. It was like falling onto a grill.

When my skin collided with the heated metal, it triggered vibrations in the surrounding air, and the sounds produced were nothing short of sizzling.

The moment of contact was explosive. My composed world melted into a chaotic nightmare of pain; my face, legs, and both hands were scorched, deeply seared with excruciating third-degree burns.

In an instant I went from inquisitive to incapacitated.

For more than a year my walker was put away. I was carried everywhere on a pillow, and my carefree pastime of exploration was replaced with three medicated baths a day.

The doctors offered little hope for my full recovery, going so far as to tell my folks not to expect much from me. They warned that I would never be as physically active as my siblings, or able to follow in the family's musical, instrumental tradition; my burned hands would never move again.

To a family whose life and living revolved around music, the doctors' declaration was a deafening blast. The unbelievable, the unacceptable, seemed unavoidable.

But there is a difference between medical and musical theory— and the world surrounding me was filled with musicians!

Sound and emotion combined produces music; it is an audible frequency that stirs the surrounding air. These vibrations are usually set in motion by a deliberate, physical act: a blast of air forced through a brass mouthpiece, or the downstroke of a piano key propelling a cushioned hammer against a tuned string. In a house filled with instruments, I was surrounded by melody, harmony, and rhythm. Yet of all these combined forms of music, the vibrations I found most moving were the sounds and emotions produced when my mother stirred the air.

When all I could do was listen, that's when Mom was the most instrumental. Her reassuring embrace, the gentle washing and exercising of my hands, her frequent whispered prayers—it was music, not just for the ears, but for the soul. Over those agonizing years of struggle, her delicate but deliberate actions consistently stirred the air around me. And eventually, Mom's melody drowned out the lingering echo of the doctors' prognosis.

That musical combination of love and faith was instrumental in my healing. Mom's vibrations changed the atmosphere and compelled me to put one foot in front of the other and learn to explore again.

With my courage stirred, my once inquisitive nature revived, and eventually I found my way onto the bench of the family piano. There, instinctively, my injured hands descended onto the keyboard. The moment of contact was magical. The smooth ivory of the keys felt good against my tender skin.

Little by little, exercising my fingers across the keys became an informal part of my therapy. Awkward notes gradually grew into melodies, those melodies transposed into chords, and in time, this once-incapacitated child transformed into what every Burger aspired to be—a musician.

When I turned five, my folks decided it was time to introduce me to a larger world. That's when Mom drove me to the big city of Chattanooga, to a building that seemed huge. Like home and the family store, the place was filled with music. But nothing I saw inside looked familiar; that is, until people I didn't know showed me a keyboard and asked me to play. That first public performance led to my acceptance into the prestigious Cadek Conservatory of Music. That day I became the youngest student in its history.

Cadek was far more than a school; the conservatory was my own personal observatory, a place where I could go to explore the unknown. There I was exposed to countless cultures, and I visited each one with the help of my new transporter, my piano—my bench with wings.

Sitting at the keyboard I toured the mind of Beethoven, examined the complexities of Bach, and marveled at the genius of Mozart. And as the years passed, my once-immovable hands became a blur, rapidly maturing with instrumental skill.

Playing the compositions of the masters was, of course, a thrill. But still nothing could move me like my mother's music—the combined four-part harmony of gospel. Its sounds and emotions were stirring. Though simple, the songs captivated me, especially at the age of nine, when I was introduced to the subject of the music—the Master of masters.

Upon discovering the One who heard my mother's prayers, I began to focus all my natural instincts on the music that explored him. Summoning my curiosity and all my developed skills, I turned my attention to studying every songbook, every hymnal, and every scrap of sheet music I could find. I wanted to learn to stir the air; not just fill it with pretty noise, but actually vibrate my surroundings with sounds capable of changing the atmosphere. Like Mom, I too wanted to be instrumental.

So in between my high school studies and conservatory concerts, I started playing for gospel groups around my small town. Those local concerts gradually led to regional conventions. That in turn opened the door to statewide appearances, and before long I was the steady, onstage accompaniment for the southern gospel group, The Celestials.

After that warm-up, I was hooked. In the time it took me to throw all my sheet music into a suitcase, I climbed aboard the legendary Kingsmen's bus, and went on to accompany their four-part harmony for thirteen years, nineteen albums, and countless miles on the road. Then, in 1993, gospel music icon Bill Gaither invited me to be part of what is now the world-renowned Gaither Vocal Band. And the rest, as they say, is history; much of which has been captured for posterity on the many award-winning *Homecoming* CDs and DVDs.

Today, when my healed hands collide with those eighty-eight ivory keys, the moment of contact is still explosive, magical, a miracle. For over thirty years I have been able to deliberately set in motion vibrations in the surrounding air, and the positive sounds produced have changed the atmosphere for all who have opened their souls and listened.

My piano, my trusty bench with wings, has allowed me to explore more worlds than my wheeled walker ever could. But the decision of which vehicle would be my transporter was not only my most painful choice, it was one that was almost made for me. That is, until my mother turned music into medicine and stirred the air of my once little world with sounds of love and faith.

Why did I have to go through all that, especially at such a young age? We may never know this side of Heaven. But as a musician I believe it has something to do with timing. For a note to be heard at a given moment, a finger must fall on a piano key early enough to allow the corresponding hammer to strike the tuned string at the precise time.

Likewise, for my piano to be heard today, maybe I had to fall on that grate early to trigger the hammer; that blow to me and my family that eventually stirred me to my assignment and tuned me to the music of God.

All I know for certain is that we all fall. And though the blows we suffer may be hard, God will never allow us to go through more than we can bear. Just look inside a piano; even the little hammers are cushioned.

Between chaos and composition, prognosis and progress, there is indeed a fine line. I stumbled over it, explored both sides of it, and made an incredible discovery: we all have a choice.

I could have lived my life being incapacitated, but I chose instead to be instrumental.

☙ PRAYER ❧

No matter what I may see or hear, let me never forget that I can change my atmosphere. I can drown out the negative noise when I deliberately stir the air with sounds of faith—that musical medicine for the soul.

❝Faith comes from hearing. ❞

ROMANS 10:17

Brian Lane Green

Tony Award nominee for Best Actor in a Musical for his performance as Spacepunk in *Starmites,* Brian Lane Green made his Broadway debut as Huck Finn in *Big River.* He went on to star in the first national tour of that show and in the national tour of Andrew Lloyd Webber's *Joseph and the Amazing Technicolor Dreamcoat.* He also appeared on Broadway as Jo Jo in the Cy Coleman musical *The Life.*

On television, Green has guest-starred on several soap operas and numerous primetime shows including *Sabrina the Teenage Witch, Murder, She Wrote, Matlock,* and *Highway to Heaven.* His film credits include starring roles in *Circuit* and *Friends and Family.*

Green can be heard on his self-titled debut CD and on the live recording of *The Words and Music of Jerry Herman: Tap Your Troubles Away, Sondheim: A Celebration at Carnegie Hall* with the Tonics, *George and Ira Gershwin: A Musical Tribute*, and *Grateful: The Songs of John Bucchino*.

Green recently made his debut as a playwright and composer with the original musical *Waiting for the Glaciers to Melt*, which was chosen to be part of New York City's Midtown International Theater Festival.

When All Else Fails

Throwing my bag over my shoulder, I hugged another dazed cast member good-bye and stepped through the backstage door, out into the Manhattan night. The run of another Broadway show was over. Now what?

Onstage, the glare of the footlights may have obscured my view of the audience; but at least there I knew where I stood, and where my next choreographed step would take me. But now, underneath the neon lights of midtown, I had no idea which way to go; I had no script for this stage of my life.

Opening-night jitters were nothing compared to the unsettling shivers of closing a show. I had known the good fortune of playing the lead in three long-running Broadway musicals. But now I was out of a job. There were no parts and no promises on the horizon. At that moment I was certain of only one thing—I would be spending the foreseeable future by myself. My three-year romance was collapsing. The final curtain was on the verge of falling.

The title on the darkened theatre marquee said it all, "*The Life*—CLOSED." I should have been stressed or, at least, gravely concerned. But I wasn't. For some unexplainable reason I was OK with it. I was calm.

A few days passed, and I found myself taking a long walk with an old friend. Although he was aware of the complexity of my plight, our conversation was sparse. The only consistent sound between us was our shoes on the sidewalk. The in-sync rhythm of our casual pace was in blatant contrast to the chaos of my life and the surrounding city. The subtlety of it was comforting, actually reassuring, and I found myself exhaling serenely. "I feel a strange sense of peace deep in my soul."

After a couple of steps, my friend turned to me, never breaking his stride. "That's beautiful. What's that from?"

"From?" I repeated, "It's not *from* anything."

"Well, it should be," he smiled. As we harmoniously weaved through the confusion of oncoming pedestrians, he added, "Sounds like the first line of a song."

That got me thinking.

Over the next day or so, as I gathered up my belongings to move to a new sublet, a sporadic flow of words began to fill my head. It was as if, along with packing my boxes, I was suddenly, subconsciously storing up phrases that contained strength. Scribbling them down wherever and whenever I could, I found myself focusing my attention more on these sudden words of encouragement than on the unscripted days that lay ahead.

I feel a strange sense of peace deep in my soul

I have a knowing that I have never known

A calm has come over me

The casual cadence of the words, the subtle self-assurance of the sentiment, sounded like my grandfather. Like me, he too had dedicated his life to the stage, but with a slight variation; his platform was a pulpit. Papaw's exceptional point of view, his innocent confidence in the surrounding world, was a rare perspective that I envied.

Confusion may be all around

And the rushing winds, they may surround me

No matter how often his storms threatened to blow him down, he faced each torrent, leaned into the wind, and in doing so always dispelled the danger of falling.

Yet I feel like the eye of a hurricane

And I'm using the storm force to ground me

I scribbled down the words as fast as they came. Even as flashes of the darkened theatre and the rising gusts of my stormy relationship swirled around me, the words kept coming. Each phrase gave me added strength. Each new line drew me closer to a more positive image; my grandfather's favorite pulpit soliloquy—the tale of a sudden storm and a small ship on the open sea . . .

When all else fails

Like a ship that has cast its sails

The crew of the wind-tossed vessel spent all of their energy trying to maintain their footing—that is, all but one man. Taking advantage of the swaying sea, this exceptional fellow curled himself up in the belly of the boat and went to sleep, as if nothing was wrong. When the terrified crew found him, their demeanor seemed almost as violent as the storm. Raising their voices above the wind they yelled, "Don't you care that we all may perish?"

The calm man quietly rose, weaved his way past his confused shipmates, stepped through the galley hatch and out into the violent night. There, facing the full force of the roaring storm, he did something amazing, unexpected; he casually spoke into the wind.

"Peace, be still." The swelling waves ebbed. The ship's sail fell limp.

His words were simple, profoundly beautiful, like the opening line of a song. Where did they come from?

Though surrounded by confusion and fear, this exceptional man would not be deterred. His point of view, like Papaw's, was enviable. Though the waves were high and the winds were gusting, the calm man, nevertheless, faced the storm. He leaned into it and dispelled the danger . . . just like Papaw.

And although he was out of step with his dazed crew and the surrounding chaotic world, he exhaled comforting words of peace as if nothing was wrong; just like . . . me.

Where did the words come from?

I was right when I told my friend that such words do not come from anything. Instead, they come from somewhere—a higher, heavenly source; a power that my grandfather could explain far better than I.

It was that source the disciples witnessed in the boat.

I am harnessing the wind to get me home again

It was that Spirit I witnessed in my grandfather's enviable life.

Riding it above the sea

It was that perspective that gave me my unexplainable calm, and helped me to lean into the storm . . .

Stealing its velocity

Using it to carry me

. . . and regain control of my ship.

I feel a strange sense of peace deep in my soul

I will experience again those opening-night jitters. And I'm sure there will be other show closings. But looking at life through calm eyes is like walking in sync with an old friend. It doesn't matter how out of step the surrounding world may be; our subtle harmony of companionship is comforting, reassuring—enviable.

Though at times my plight may be complex, I'm OK with it because, like Papaw, I know where that innocent confidence, that peace, comes from. And I am grateful.

I have a knowing that I have never known

A calm has come over me

⊗ Prayer ⊗

Choreograph my every step, so we can walk together like friends. And teach me how to hear your calming voice, especially over the wind.

> "Thou wilt keep him in perfect peace, whose mind is stayed on thee."

ISAIAH 26:3 (*KJV*)

Calm

❧ WORDS AND MUSIC BY BRIAN LANE GREEN ❧

I feel a strange sense of peace deep
in my soul
I have a knowing that I have never
known
A calm has come over me
A calm has come over me

Confusion may be all around
And the rushing winds, they may
surround me
Yet I feel like the eye of a hurricane
And I'm using the storm force to
ground me

When all else fails
Like a ship that has cast its sails
I am harnessing the wind to get me
home again
Riding it above the sea
Stealing its velocity
Using it to carry me

I feel a strange sense of peace deep
in my soul
I have a knowing that I have never
known
A calm . . .
A calm has come over me

David
Phelps

David Phelps's gift was noticed by his family and local church members when he was just a boy in Tomball, Texas. He became the youngest winner of Christian music's Seminar in the Rockies competition in 1988. After earning a music degree from Baylor University, he took the position of Artist-in-Residence at First Baptist Church in Hurst, Texas. His fresh sound then attracted the world's spotlight upon his becoming part of the legendary Gaither Vocal Band.

Over the last decade, David has recorded six award-winning Gaither Vocal Band CDs, five critically acclaimed solo offerings, and over forty certified gold and platinum Gaither *Homecoming* collections. His work with the Gaither Vocal Band has also brought him four Dove Awards and two Grammy Awards.

His wife, Lori, helps David balance his roles as acclaimed vocalist and down-to-earth husband and father of four. She homeschools the children in order to let them spend more time with their father as they go on the road to nearly 150 concert appearances every year. When not traveling, David and his family reside in middle Tennessee.

The Power to Stay

Singing is easy; being away from home—that's hard.

Every time I pack for a concert tour and have to kiss my family good-bye, it's difficult; for I know there is a fine line between "going away" and "leaving." Although I'm absent for just a few days at a time, I try to make sure, before I go, that my wife and kids know that each one is truly loved; that they are my five dearest reasons for living. And that when I'm on the road, I'm working . . . not leaving.

From the platform of the Baptist church my granddad pastored, to the stage of Carnegie Hall performing with the Gaither Vocal Band, I have spent my life traveling, singing about the staying power of God's love. That theme of divine constancy has been a reoccurring chorus with me, all the way back to my childhood.

Back then, along with mandatory piano lessons, my parents made sure that my sisters and I never missed church. Every time the doors opened we were consistently there, harmonizing "Jesus loves me, this I know." Back then, the staying power of the word "love" never really hit me. That is, until the word "leaving" started hitting a little too close to home.

True, we were in church every time the doors opened. But at our house, behind closed doors, my harmonious family was in discord. My mother's childhood had not been as pleasant as the world she had created for my sisters and me. When the memories of those not-so-good days surfaced, Mom would battle against them the only way she knew how; by letting loose a verbal volley in the direction of the only adult available, Dad.

Wounded by a past she couldn't forget, Mom's only defense was lashing out. But though her words were often loud, Dad did his best to understand her pain. They were two wonderful parents, who loved their family and each other dearly. But the situation had them teetering on the line between drifting apart and leaving.

Back then singing was fun; waiting for the other shoe to drop wasn't.

Finally, the unmentionable was acknowledged while on a road trip in the family car. My two sisters and I were in the backseat, Mom sat in the front, and as usual, Dad was driving. As we journeyed down the road and the car wheels whirled, so did my mother's memories. Inevitably, the music wafting from the radio was soon drowned out by loud voices blaring from the front seat. After enduring a few miles of this, Dad pulled off onto the road's shoulder and Mom stormed out of the car, slamming the passenger door behind her. In an unexpected instant all was quiet. A tense moment ticked by. Then my older sister, squirming a little in her seat, finally broke the silence.

"Dad," she spoke up with a surprising tone of maturity, "why don't you just . . . leave her?"

The words stunned me—everyone. There's something about saying what you feel, out loud, that makes the thought, the possibility, real. The notion seemed logical, terrifying, necessary, and absolutely unimaginable!

For a long moment Dad didn't move. He just sat there staring straight ahead, contemplating the question. Then, finally turning around in the seat, he faced us. And in a soft, gentle voice I will never forget he replied, "Honey, when you love someone, you don't leave."

It's the dream you give up for someone else

It's being strong when you're weak yourself

Though it tears you up you trust again

Hatred loses and forgiveness wins

Years passed. My solo career began to take off. And as I hit the road, like the lyrics of an unforgettable song, Dad's words followed me. When I met Lori, and discovered that I loved her too much to live without her, I heard the words. When I held each of my four children the first time and felt my heart fall into rhythm with theirs, Dad's reply echoed in my ears. And every time we thought that Mom and Dad had finally come to the end of their road, the impasse was broken by the sentiment of those words, spoken out loud, making the possibility of reconciliation real.

You turn your cheek when you want to fight

Sell all you have and lay down your life

And when hope is gone

You're the one who keeps holding on

The turning point came at Easter. My folks, now grandparents, had traveled to Dallas to attend my holiday concert. Once more the family was all together inside the open doors of a church celebrating the resurrection of Christ, and the staying power of his love. After the last crescendo, the proud grandparents embraced their still growing brood. Then they set off back to Houston, on another road trip.

Texas is a big state and the journey from one city to another, even these days, is measured in long hours. As the van's headlights illuminated the road, it was just the two of them now; Mom in the passenger's seat dozing, and Dad, as usual, driving. The only sound between them was the whirling of the wheels.

Then, in an unexpected instant, Mom suddenly woke from her slumber. It wasn't the startling recurrence of an old memory that forced her eyes open, but rather the loud, high-pitched shatter of the windshield. As she emerged from her daze all she could see was a blur of glass. But her ears distinctly heard my father's voice declare, "I'm gone!"

Grabbing the abandoned steering wheel at 70 mph, Mom struggled to keep the wheels on the road. Bravely, she forced herself into the driver's seat, practically sitting on Dad's limp, bloody frame. Fighting wind, glass, and every emotion one could possibly imagine, she pushed the wounded vehicle to its limits and searched for the nearest hospital.

As she drove, all she could hear was my father's declaration, "I'm gone." The words stunned her. Hearing it spoken out loud—the threat that had haunted their marriage for years—made the possibility all too real. Glancing over at his injured face, the notion seemed inevitable, unbelievable . . . and far from what she wanted.

It's the only thing worth life and death

It's the first moment and the final breath

It's a broken heart keeping a solemn vow

And a lost soul being found

At the hospital the prognosis wasn't promising. What was first suspected as a gunshot turned out to be the pointed antler of a buck. The large animal had been attempting to cross the road when the van's fast-approaching headlights frightened him. The deer tried to jump the van. But instead, it crashed through the windshield, propelling one of its horns through Dad's face. Immediately he was airlifted to Houston, where famed surgeon Red Duke was waiting to perform emergency surgery.

As the helicopter lifted into the air, Mom stood on the ground wondering if Dad was going away, or leaving. For the first time in years, watching Dad disappear into the night sky, Mom was alone.

You pray for faith when it's hard to believe

You choose to stay when it's easy to leave

And when hope is gone

You're the one who keeps holding on

In those first pensive hours without him, as we all hurried to be with her, Mom's mind did not dwell on the distant past she couldn't change. Instead, she rested in the unwavering grace of the Easter we had just celebrated.

Entering the church within her heart, where the doors are always open, she appealed to the Love that never leaves; the Love that even defied death to keep that vow. To him she pleaded for mercy—not for the past, but for the future. She prayed that the love that had stuck with her all these years would stick around just a little longer.

It's reaching out and holding on so someone else will know

Love is in the not letting go

A whole decade of Easters have passed since then. Dad is as good as new. Now in their sixties, I watch my parents with amazement. They're like teenagers, always holding hands. They stuck it out. They stuck together. While many modern families are fragmented versions of themselves, with grandparents having to schedule appointments to see their grandchildren separately, my folks are enjoying the love of their family and the harmony of their still growing brood, together. And we are still enjoying them.

That's what love is

When you give until there's nothing left

And it makes you give your very best

That's what love is

It can make you laugh and make you cry

It can let you down and lift you up so high

When you find the only reason left to live

That's what love is

Every time I pack for a concert tour and kiss Lori, Callie, Maggie, Grant, and Coby good-bye, I remember Dad's words and make sure I tell them, "I'll be right back."

Traveling, singing about God's staying power is rewarding. But returning to a house filled with love—that's coming home!

✂ PRAYER ✂

Let me never forget the sacrifice you made for me on the cross. You could have called ten thousand angels. But you loved me . . . and didn't leave.

> "For I am convinced that neither death nor life, neither angels nor demons, neither the present nor the future, nor any powers, neither height nor depth, nor anything else in all creation, will be able to separate us from the love of God that is in Christ Jesus our Lord."
>
> ROMANS 8:38, 39

That's What Love Is

BY DAVID PHELPS, TYLER HAYES-BIECK, AND GREG BIECK

It's the only thing worth life
and death
It's the first moment and the
final breath
It's a broken heart keeping a
solemn vow
And a lost soul being found
You pray for faith when it's hard
to believe
You choose to stay when it's easy
to leave
And when hope is gone you're the
one who keeps holding on

Chorus:
That's what love is
When you give until there's
nothing left
And it makes you give your very best
That's what love is
It can make you laugh and make
you cry
It can let you down and lift you up
so high
When you find the only reason left
to live
That's what love is

It's the dream you give up for
someone else
It's being strong when you're weak
yourself
Though it tears you up you
trust again
Hatred loses and forgiveness wins
You turn your cheek when you want
to fight
Sell all you have and lay down
your life
And when hope is gone you're the
one who keeps holding on

Repeat Chorus

It's reaching out and holding on so
someone else will know
Love is in the not letting go

Repeat Chorus

Kelly
Minter

Virginia native Kelly Minter's deep-rooted spiritual heritage has helped to shape her latest creative endeavors. She gives special credit to her father, Pastor Mike Minter (the highly regarded host of Salem XM Radio's broadcast "Compelling Truth"), for building that Christian foundation.

Though she once dreamed of being a basketball star, Kelly's talents in songwriting and performing brought her into the Christian music scene in the late 90s. Her strong debut in 2001, *Good Day*, led her to tour with such artists as Bebo Norman, Sonicflood, and Watermark. She later signed with the Here to Him label of Cross Driven Records and linked up with Margaret Becker to produce her 2003 release, *Wrestling the Angels*.

A multi-faceted talent, Kelly also became a published author with her book, *Water into Wine* (WaterBrook Press, 2004). With this project, she hopes to shed light on what she calls "the hopeful struggle" we all face in our Christian walks. Kelly has also been involved with World Vision tours to Africa and continues to be blessed by her experiences of servanthood there.

Long Nights, a Tall Ladder, and a Good Grip

I was living every composer's dream. I finally had a record deal.

I had resisted the urge to move to Nashville until my contract was carved in stone. But now that it was signed and sealed, I was settling in. I traded in my Virginia driver's license, put Tennessee tags on the car, and began tuning up for my first solo collection. I had made it. I was officially living and composing in Music City.

But no sooner had I unpacked and mailed in my change-of-address form, than the news reached me. My record label was gone! Out of nowhere it was bought out, taken over; the corporation dissolved. Just like that, my freshly-inked recording deal was no more.

The news hit me where I lived—literally. I was now stranded in the middle of Nashville, with no visible means of support. The sudden uncertainty of it all had me wrestling with the timing of the decision, the gravity of the situation, and the unexplainable logic of another's free will. And in a flash of down-to-earth reality I was suddenly living every composer's nightmare. I was disappointed, confused, and far from composed. What could I do? The answer was painful, but obvious—anything but give up.

So I set out to do whatever was necessary. I ran errands, did odd jobs. For well over a year, as I painted walls and mowed monotonous mazes in the neighbor's lawn, I tried to make sense out of the crazy pattern of my life. As the mower's engine turned the rotary blades, I continually turned over in my spinning mind the most obvious question: *Lord, why did you bring me here—for this?*

It was a lonely experience, but though my family was far away, I did not go through this alone. In Nashville I was surrounded by a family of friends; among them, the amazing Margaret Becker. A composer, like me, Maggie understood intimately the maze I was struggling to navigate. And whether she was consciously aware of it or not, she helped me to put things in perspective.

On a visit with her one day, she pulled out a page of scribbled lyrics. And asking for my opinion, she read them out loud:

I'm wrestling the angels, and maybe I won't win

But if this is how the blessings flow then count me in

I'm falling on your mercy, I am losing to gain

Walking with the evidence of change

When she looked up from the page she could see that I was in tears. "Was it *that* bad?"

"No," I tried to smile. "I love it . . . I can relate."

The lyrics hinted at the Old Testament story of Jacob. Like me, he had packed up all he owned and left home to find his land of promise. Like me, he had seen his share of dreams, nightmares, disappointments, and contractual disputes. And in a situation reminiscent of my own, Jacob found himself alone, struggling to figure out what the next uncertain day would bring.

I could definitely relate. Seeing the recognition in my teary eyes, Maggie invited me to help her finish the song. And after some thought, the words spilled out.

This is what I'm thinking

I'm a little out of step

My spirit's leaning right

But the living keeps on pulling to the left

Living—it's just another way of saying "enduring the struggle." Every day we wrestle with gravity, time, and the free will of others. It is a perpetual battle for survival that will continue as long as we are aware of our surroundings and care about right and wrong.

I'm thoroughly conflicted

Got a pebble in my shoe

I wanna have it my way

But I wanna come out looking more like you

As the words came to me, I realized that we all just want a quick fix. If we each had a magic wand, no doubt we would zap ourselves some fast cash and a limo ride down Easy Street. We would deliberately avoid the struggles of the race and opt for a fast shortcut to reach the finish line first, without ever breaking a sweat.

I realized that the destination is all that seems to matter. Whether it be crossing the finish line or signing on the record label's dotted line—getting there and staying there, as easily as possible, has become the goal; the end-all and be-all of living. But deep down we all know (and occasionally need reminding that) life doesn't work that way. There is no such thing as Easy Street.

If our heavenly home is our only real goal, then why did God put us on earth first?

Jacob didn't dream of an escalator to Heaven. He didn't envision an elevator, or a Star Trek transporter that would beam him through the pearly gates. Jacob saw a ladder. He saw a process that required both individual will and a deliberate effort in order to reach that ultimate destination.

There is something about "the struggle" that makes us who we are. And that fight begins as early as the threshold of birth. That first struggle to reach the light at the end of the tunnel must be some kind of final training exercise informing us that, to reach life's destinations, our will and spiritual vigor must work together and persevere.

If anyone understood the physical and spiritual strength that comes from this struggle, it was Jacob. Maybe it was that initial fight he and his brother Esau had inside his mother's womb. Or it could have been their endless battles over everything from birthrights to soup. But Jacob's journey certainly suggests that he learned well the tactic of "keepin' on," despite the disappointments or the height of the ladder. He knew that no goal was reachable without expending both faith and physical effort.

All alone on that dark night, pondering the next day's uncertain confrontation with his fraternal twin, Jacob wrestled with the patterns of his life. He thought about the timing of Esau's birth, just before his own, and of the nightmare that was caused by their contractual dispute. He contemplated the gravity of their reunion and grappled with the volatile history of his brother's free will.

Far from composed, he knew that the road to reconciliation would be no Easy Street. And as he considered the down-to-earth reality of it all, no doubt his spinning mind wrestled with the obvious question, *Lord, why did you bring me here—for this?*

On that eerie evening of self-evaluation, his thoughts likely included the memory of a similar dark night, years before, when he was likewise alone.

After his father's passing, after Esau's dinner-time deal that all but dissolved the family business, Jacob left home and journeyed off by himself. Feeling abandoned, as if he had no visible means of support, he camped alone on a hillside. Resting his head on a pillow of stone, he closed his eyes. But as the lonely man fell asleep, he discovered that he was not alone.

In a dream, Jacob was shown an enormous ladder. Its countless rungs reached from the ground up to the clouds and beyond. And on this heavenly ladder were angels both ascending and descending. In this vision, near the top of the towering structure, Jacob saw God. And a voice called down to him and declared, "I am the LORD, the God of your father Abraham and the God of Isaac. I will give you and your descendants the land on which you are lying. . . . I am with you and will watch over you wherever you go, and I will bring you back to this land. I will not leave you" (Genesis 28:13-15).

The words were reassuring, a promise that Jacob could depend on. It was a divine contract that could never be bought out. It was a solid deal on which he could rest assured. And as a testament to that confident rest, Jacob marked the moment in stone, using the very rock he had used as his pillow.

As that pleasant, long-ago memory flashed across his mind, a sudden intrusion of reality brought him back to the moment, back to that dark night. Before his wide-awake eyes, he saw an actual angel. It was no apparition, no stone pillow dream. Like life itself, Jacob's unexpected visitor was a down-to-earth reality, staring him in the face.

Whether the angel's visit was meant to be a comfort, or just a tangible reminder of God's promise, I don't know. But if Jacob was feeling that night the way I was feeling that day visiting

Margaret, the reassuring touch of a friend's hand would have been more than a comfort, it would have been a necessity—a blessing worth reaching for. And if that friend was an emissary from the Land of Promise, I too would have grabbed on and not let go until I heard a lyrical blessing, spoken out loud.

"Jacob replied, 'I will not let you go unless you bless me'" (Genesis 32:26). The wrestling match had lasted all night. This time he wasn't holding on to his brother's foot, but instead he was holding tight to one of God's footmen. He was struggling as we all do to keep on keepin' on, toward the final destination.

His vast experience with life's struggles gave him the internal will to do anything and everything—but give up. The odds were against him (after all he was going one-on-one with an angel), but Jacob stayed in the fight. He took his lumps, but never threw in the towel. And even when the heavenly emissary gave him a limp, the man didn't let go until he got his blessing.

The end result of Jacob's long night of struggle was—change. As the light of a new day was about to dawn, he heard the angel proclaim words of transformation—among them a new name, Israel. That change managed to affect every facet of his life. In fact before the sun went down on that very day, Jacob and Esau embraced as brothers. They resolved their old contract dispute and set in motion a complete reorganization of the family business.

Jacob's story hit me right where I lived. I had endured my share of struggles and dark lonely nights of the soul. The year and a half I spent running errands and mowing lawns may not have been as dramatic as wrestling an angel, but it took all of my internal will and spiritual vigor to maintain a good grip. But the journey was made a little easier thanks to visits with heaven-sent emissaries like my friend, Margaret Becker.

Jacob's lyrical words, recorded in Genesis, illustrate both the struggles we all face every day and the transformation we can each attain, if we are willing to do anything and everything—but give up.

I can definitely relate. These days, I am back on track, living every composer's dream. And like Jacob, my journey too is recorded, in the words and music of every composition.

This is how I'm moving

It's a limp that's all my own

On this journey of becoming

On it I am sure I'm not alone

Wrestling with gravity, time, and the free will of others is draining, but the experience never fails to produce unexpected strength. Grappling with the awareness of right, wrong, and the uncertainty of tomorrow may leave us disappointed and sometimes permanently scarred, but the experience always imparts wisdom. And that vigor used to wrestle and grapple brings about maturity and change.

Change that makes a diamond out of coal

Change that makes your glory shine through these holes

The kind of change that helps you to move up another rung on Jacob's ladder.

⚜ PRAYER ⚜

You put me in this world to grow, to exercise my faith with every challenge. Though I may often feel alone in the struggle, and long for the fast lane of Easy Street, let me never forget that the light at the end of the tunnel is not the gold of Heaven's boulevard—it's you.

> "Then the man said, 'Let me go, for it is daybreak.' But Jacob replied, 'I will not let you go unless you bless me.'. . . Then the man said, 'Your name will no longer be Jacob, but Israel, because you have struggled with God and with men and have overcome.'"

GENESIS 32:26-28

Wrestling the Angels

⸮ BY MARGARET BECKER AND KELLY MINTER ⸮

This is what I'm thinking
I'm a little out of step
My spirit's leaning right
But the living keeps on pulling
    to the left

I'm thoroughly conflicted
Got a pebble in my shoe
I wanna have it my way
But I wanna come out looking more
    like you

I'm wrestling the angels, and maybe
    I won't win
But if this is how the blessings flow
    then count me in
I'm falling on your mercy, I am
    losing to gain
Walking with the evidence of
    change

This is how I'm moving
It's a limp that's all my own
On this journey of becoming
On it I am sure I'm not alone

I'm wrestling the angels, and maybe
    I won't win
But if this is how the blessings flow
    then count me in
I'm falling on your mercy, I am
    losing to gain
Walking with the evidence of
    change

Change that makes a diamond
    out of coal
Change that makes your glory shine
    through these holes

George Rowe

Born in New Jersey as Keewah Ly Eickelberger, the baby who would become George Rowe III was immediately given up for adoption and placed in Newark's foster care system. Sadly, he landed at first with an abusive, neglectful family and by the time he was fourteen months old, he was lying in a hospital bed, not expected to live. But George Rowe, Jr. and his wife, Ida, wanted to adopt him. As George tells it, "My parents visited me in the hospital, and after seeing how thin and frail I was, just wept. . . . For the first time in my young life, I went home. . . . They saved me. I have a deeper understanding of my relationship with God that parallels my relationship with my parents."

As he grew up in the small town of Clayton, New Jersey, George's life was filled with church. His grandfather was a preacher, and the family attended services every Sunday morning and night, and Wednesday night as well. And though music, like church, was always in his life, it wasn't his first career choice. George graduated on a full scholarship from Pepperdine University's School of Law. But during that final year at Pepperdine, George and his wife, Merritt, realized that being an attorney was just not what he was called to do. Something was missing.

That something was found in music. In performing, George found he could be used to touch people's lives in a way that no court case could do. He signed with Rocketown Records and then released his debut CD, *Think About That*, in December, 2003. George lives in Nashville, Tennessee, with his wife and three children—Ireland, Addyson, and Jake.

Don't Swerve

No one in my family had ever gone to college. Yet I graduated from Malibu, California's Pepperdine University on a full scholarship. It was a free ride I couldn't turn down. By everyone's standards I was on my way, traveling down the right road. . . . It just didn't seem like I was headed in the right direction.

What I had accomplished was amazing; I had beaten the odds, managed to earn a degree, and actually become a lawyer. But what I could not manage was to love my job, the law, to the same degree as I did music. But then, who gets to live *that* dream? (Other than every famous face I saw in Malibu.)

For years I split my time between daily diamond-lane commutes to my estate planning office, and my weekend road trips to do what I enjoyed most—singing. But after a million monotonous miles of switching lanes, back and forth, I realized I was getting nowhere, very slowly.

Diversion is an easy road

Down the hill and wide

But if you choose to go that route

It'll lead to your demise

My wife, Merritt, could see it. My three small children could sense it. As I straddled those two lanes, the world was passing us by. We were traveling down a wide freeway that didn't seem very free. And none of us cared enough about the destination to ask, Are we there yet? But other questions did come to mind. Why are we juggling two lives? Why are we not committing to one . . . yet feel so tied to the other?

Wisdom is a wilderness

You will make your map

Starting from Experience

Takin' Knowledge as your path

This lawyer's family needed counsel! Our lack of answers brought our wandering to a screeching halt. Standing still, trying to regain our bearings, we called on our valued friends for direction. Then, after we had done all we could to stand, we knelt.

And everything you need to know

Is written in the Book

But knowledge without some action is

Like a shoe without a foot

After plenty of prayer, we decided that if we were going to get anywhere, I would have to stop commuting. I gave up the day job. I put down my attaché case and stopped my practice. Then I picked up my instrument case and started practicing. We had picked a path and begun our journey.

Needless to say it wasn't a free ride, and the road was far from smooth. Every bump and pothole was an education. Along the way there were times when I thought back to Pepperdine and how I'd beat the odds. And I admit that on occasion I wondered if my life of music would ever reach such a degree that it would surpass my law degree. More than I ever thought I would, I found myself depending on God.

Understanding who you are

With the Savior on your side

Is one step in the right direction and

One day you'll be wise

The unemployment pavement was hard. Singing for our supper became way too real. Having doors slammed in my face wasn't fun. But giving up was not an option. This was my family, my future, a case I could not afford to lose. Learning how to be strong and stay strong was a test of faith I never would have experienced filing a legal brief.

Wisdom is supreme

So don't forget it

Understanding isn't cheap

But it's worth it

It wasn't easy. Feeding my family as well as my creativity was a constant struggle. Every day was a test of our love, trust, and patience.

There's a price you're gonna pay

Yeah, I'll admit it

You can't go left or right

Keep his path in your sight

And don't swerve

Don't swerve

Day, after week, after month, we stayed the course and continued on the road, playing concerts. One evening after completing my last set in a Nashville venue, the father-in-law of a Rocketown Records executive asked for one of my CDs; actually, it was a copy of some poor quality demos. But it was that CD, along with some diligent follow-up, that finally tipped the scales in favor of the verdict that I had lobbied for so long.

After two hard years my lesson-filled journey brought me and my family not to the end of the road, but to the beginning of my career—the launching pad of Rocketown.

If you walk with the Father

Moving mountains along the way

And listen to his leading

Your path will be straight

Before I knew it I was on a tour with Michael W. Smith, Mercy Me, and Amy Grant. Late one night, as our caravan of tour buses rolled down the highway, I couldn't sleep. My mind was reeling, trying to imagine what road I would've been on if I had given up and let my faith swerve. But here I was—I had beaten the odds, again. I had managed not only to earn a degree in law, but to raise my love of music to an even higher degree. And who gets to live *that* dream? (Every famous face I saw on the bus.)

As I sat pondering all this, Michael W. plopped down in the seat beside me. He couldn't sleep either. We got to talking about the life we'd chosen; that road so rarely taken. And listening to him I realized what a privilege it was to communicate, with our words and music, the experiences that lead us all closer to God and each other.

That night we pulled out our wallets and bragged about our wives and kids. And with a smile I told Michael that no one in my family had ever gone to college. But the lessons we learned together on our way to Rocketown had made us all "road scholars."

⊰ Prayer ⊱

Only you know the path I should take. Lead the way. Never let me stray. When I am confused, help me to stand. And if I am too weary to stand, grant me the grace to kneel.

66 Get wisdom, get understanding;
do not forget my words or swerve from them. 99

PROVERBS 4:5

Swerve

{ WORDS AND MUSIC BY GEORGE ROWE AND BRIAN STECKLER {

Chorus:
Wisdom is supreme
So don't forget it
Understanding isn't cheap
But it's worth it
There's a price you're gonna pay
Yeah, I'll admit it
You can't go left or right
Keep his path in your sight
And don't swerve
Don't swerve

Wisdom is a wilderness
You will make your map
Starting from Experience
Takin' Knowledge as your path
And everything you need to know
Is written in the Book
But knowledge without some
    action is
Like a shoe without a foot

Diversion is an easy road
Down the hill and wide
But if you choose to go that route
It'll lead to your demise
Understanding who you are
With the Savior on your side
Is one step in the right direction and
One day you'll be wise

Bridge:
If you walk with the Father
Moving mountains along the way
And listen to his leading
Your path will be straight

Kyla Rowland

Kyla Rowland is known as one of the all-time greatest song-writers in the history of southern gospel music. Born and raised the daughter of a Baptist preacher and a church pianist, living for Christ just came naturally to her. She continues her walk today through songwriting, speaking engagements, and singing. She performs with her husband, Bob Mullins, as Kyla Rowland and Deliverance, and they are often joined by her son and daughter-in-law, Barry and Tammy Rowland.

Not long ago Kyla was honored with a special tribute album on which many of today's top southern gospel artists recorded popular songs that she has written through the years. Kyla has received more Songwriter of the Year nominations from *Singing News* than any female writer to date. Her songs, many of which have reached top five on the charts and have received Dove Award and Song of the Year nominations, have been recorded by such artists as Gold City, the Cathedrals, the Kingsmen, the Hoskins Family, the Inspirations, the Cookes, the Perrys, and many more.

Kyla is also a book author. Her first book, *Between Me and the Storm*, was published in 2002. She has since authored two other titles, *Everyday Life* and *Girl Talk*. Her fourth book, *This Song's for You*, is a compilation of fifty of her most beloved songs and the stories behind them.

Safe Thus Far

You could call me a fraud. Many of my songs are just my mother, Eulalia, set to music and rhyme.

Back in 1984, my children were almost grown, and the anticipation of that freedom had my husband and I making plans. As the time neared for our hatchlings to leave the nest, we too were ready for new adventures—eager to see more of the world. But as our children set off to try their wings, and Bob and I packed our bags, preparing to do likewise, my widowed mother arrived.

She had nowhere else to go. And as we embraced at the door I realized, neither did I.

The prospect of freedom I was so looking forward to experiencing vanished when she set down her bags. The timing seemed all wrong. I was ready to go. She was ready to stay. I was ready to experience life on a whole new level. And though I didn't realize it at the time, God was ready to help—just not the way I expected.

Eulalia moved in with us. And I set my bags and my dreams of freedom off in the corner.

There was no middle ground with Mother. When you were in Eulalia's presence you either laughed, cried, or praised God. She had a power in her that was almost tangible. This little warrior walked on water, walked through fire, and prayed prayers that caused grown men to tremble. Every day with her was another adventure.

For twenty years, living under our roof, I watched her touch every life that passed by. And though I eyed my bags a time or two, Mother showed me a world beyond any I could've visited.

That notion finally hit home on a memorable afternoon as I sat in a recliner next to hers. Aging and ill, Mother had been in great pain all day. And I had already given her all the medication I dared.

"Hang on, Mother. In a couple of hours you can have another pill."

"Oh, I'm all right," she whispered bravely.

But watching her, listening to her softly groan, I felt as though I was the one in pain. I just could not understand why a precious, faithful servant like Eulalia had to experience *this* part of life. How many times had I heard her plead the cause of others and witnessed glorious deliverance? The timing seemed all wrong. I wasn't ready for her to go. And given her pain, I wasn't sure she wanted to stay. I needed answers. And though I didn't realize it at the time, God was ready to help—just not the way I expected.

Looking over at me she whispered, "Let's pray."

Wonderful! I knew mother had only to bow her head, as always, and both of us would be instantly transported into heavenly places. If anyone could pray this thing away, she could. Bowing and closing my eyes, I waited for the sweet relief I knew would come.

"Lord," her voiced raised a little, "for all the times you've come to my rescue, for being my dearest, most beloved companion these eighty-three years, I praise your name . . . and I want to thank you for bringing me safe thus far."

Not once did she ask God to touch her pain. She only wanted to thank him for the journey. That's when it hit me. Living with Eulalia I was living my dream; experiencing life on a whole new level. And as soon as she whispered "Amen," I moved to the piano.

∽

Just came from the throne room today, been talking with him

I was reminded where I am and where I've been

I've sailed many waters rough and deep

But someone has sailed each one with me

Safely and surely I rode the storms with my dearest friend

∽

As the words flowed, all my old baggage disappeared, for I realized that God had taken me on a journey far better than any adventure Bob and I could have planned. My widowed mother, who had nowhere else to go, was the tour guide. And the creator of all we surveyed had been with us, watching over us, the whole time.

Oh, I am safe thus far, he's brought me safe thus far

I'm in the ship with one who made the moon and stars

I praise him for mercy that can't fail

I love that old grace that still prevails

This is my story, I give him the glory

Safe thus far

As Eulalia rested in the comfort of her recliner, I sat at the piano and thought about the days to come.

I've smiled in the face of stormy seas as they rolled apart

I've rested in peace as he spoke to my trembling heart

I really don't know what lies ahead

But I have no doubt, no fear, nor dread

I'll still be standing, telling this story

Safe thus far

Many of my songs are just my mother, Eulalia, set to music and rhyme. The lyrics are simple, but the lessons learned are profound.

Your life will never truly begin until you set down your bags and leave the planning up to God. He is always there, always ready to help—though it might not be the way you expect.

Disappointments and questions are inevitable, but he is always able. I know because he has seen Eulalia, and me, safe thus far.

◁ PRAYER ▷

Let me learn to praise you, to trust you, even in the midst of pain.

66 But he said to me, 'My grace is sufficient for you, for my power is made perfect in weakness.' Therefore I will boast all the more gladly about my weaknesses, so that Christ's power may rest on me. 99

2 CORINTHIANS 12:9

Safe Thus Far

⸲ WORDS AND MUSIC BY KYLA ROWLAND ⸲

Just came from the throne room
today, been talking with him
I was reminded where I am and
where I've been
I've sailed many waters rough
and deep
But someone has sailed each one
with me
Safely and surely I rode the storms
with my dearest friend

Oh, I am safe thus far, he's brought
me safe thus far
I'm in the ship with one who made
the moon and stars
I praise him for mercy that can't fail
I love that old grace that still prevails
This is my story, I give him the glory
Safe thus far

I've smiled in the face of stormy seas
As they rolled apart
I've rested in peace as he spoke
To my trembling heart
I really don't know what lies ahead
But I have no doubt, no fear,
nor dread
I'll still be standing, telling this story
Safe thus far

Mark Schultz

Adopted at the age of two weeks old, singer/songwriter Mark Schultz grew up in Colby, Kansas, where he became a successful athlete. However, his musical talent was even greater, and it led him to move to Nashville. His music career didn't begin right away, as he first ended up in youth ministry at First Presbyterian Church. But his position there served as inspiration. (In fact, Schultz says he still writes songs only at what he calls "The Chapel," a music room in the church.)

Soon, weekly concerts featuring Mark's talents were drawing crowds and attention from the music industry. Eventually, he signed with Myrrh Records, and released his self-titled debut album in 2000.

Since then he's had half a dozen No. 1 songs and over three times that number of awards and nominations. His latest project, *Mark Schultz Live: A Night of Stories and Songs* (CD/DVD), won him his first Dove Award in 2006 for Long Form Music Video of the Year. It contains his greatest hits and reveals the stories behind each of the songs, displaying why this artist has been described as Christian music's premier storyteller.

Writing on the Wall

If one picture paints a thousand words, then the framed composition said far more than a thousand paintings. Though not a landscape, the rendering displayed an all–encompassing view. Though not a portrait, its colorful shapes projected a clear profile of the subject. In short, it was a masterpiece of simplicity; a poster frame filled with—words: *Elohim, El Elyon, Adonai . . .*

The wall poster was a permanent fixture in the church youth department where I served as director for eight years. No matter where you stood in the large room the prominent exhibit had the ability to catch your eye. No matter how often you read the artful arrangement, the words seemed comforting: *Yahweh, Father, Jehovah-Jireh . . .*

It was a mirror reflecting the truth, a treasure map pointing the way. The writing on the church wall was a collection of answers to whatever question might be posed.

"Why does God need so many names?" a kid in my youth group once joked, pointing to the poster.

"He doesn't," I smiled back. "God knows how infinite he is. *We* are the ones who need constant reminding." The echo of my answer took me off guard. Like the lyrics of a song, my comment on the poster struck some internal chord, and it's never stopped reverberating.

Through the years that inner echo and that wall of names both etched their way ever deeper into my subconscious and, over time, I was compelled to start composing a few reminders of my own. Eventually, when I could no longer suppress the urge, I stepped outside the church walls, mounted a concert stage and turned the spotlight of my music onto the themes of that memorable poster.

My transformation from youth director to songwriter has been an illuminating journey. Taking the stage, I discovered that God's abundance is a difficult thing to describe, no matter how many adjectives I use. Yet, living on the road, I found that all of humanity can be summed up with a single word—*wanting*.

Basically, we are all squirrels with a daily quota of needs to fill—that includes me. My nutty obsession? Almonds. I never leave home without them.

When my band and I are on the road, normal human nature tends to ratchet up a notch. Crammed on a bus and bound by a tour schedule that would confound the time-travel theories of Einstein, our squirrelly side inevitably kicks in. Mine appeared when our road manager forgot to pick up a few items at the store.

Upon hearing that our supplies were running low, my senses went on full alert. Realizing that my cache of snacks would soon be pillaged by my fellow hunter-gatherers, I squirreled away my roasted almonds and ricotta cheese; stuffing them ingeniously behind my bus bunk pillow.

Several times during the night, I awoke to the sound of footsteps. Certain that my companions had turned into a pack of hungry insomniacs, I pulled my bag of goodies deeper under the covers and suppressed the urge to announce, "No roasted almonds down here, please move along!!" The surrender of my precious stash was not an option.

The next morning, feeling more myself again, I made my way to the front of the bus for some coffee. After taking a few sips I realized I was surrounded by a band of grown men trying on tube socks! And if that wasn't strange enough, my sound guy, armed with a black marker, was actually writing numbers on the bottoms of his, to keep better track of them.

Taking in this strange sight, I flashed on my own nutty behavior a few hours earlier, and the combined scenes freeze-framed in my head. If one picture can paint a thousand words, then this snapshot said more about human nature than I could have ever imagined.

In that flash of enlightenment I could clearly see how needy, how constantly wanting we mortals truly are. Crammed into this world and seemingly bound by its limitations, we obsess like squirrels over the ever-approaching winter of the unknown, and spend our brief existence hoarding all we can.

I could barely believe my eyes, not to mention our lack of insight. Every night when the curtain goes up, we crank up the volume and proclaim the infinite abundance of God. Yet when the curtain falls, we hoard our socks and hide our snacks like there's no tomorrow (or an Almighty Father capable of providing for our needs).

The mental picture caught me off guard. And the comment I had once made about the poster reverberated again. *God knows how infinite he is. We are the ones who need constant reminding.*

How quickly we forget . . .

The Old Testament widow living during the famine had it far worse than us. The limitations of her starving world left the woman with no option but to prepare one final meal for herself and her son. But just as she was scraping the bottom of the barrel, the hungry prophet Elijah knocked on her door and boldly asked to be fed—first. The famished mother could have hidden her last handful of grain under a pillow . . . but she didn't. The prophet's brazen request reminded her of God's ability to provide, and that she had another option.

Is it so hard to remember that the first followers of Christ endured limitations we could never abide? When Jesus sent out his disciples two by two, they deliberately hit the road with only one coat and no money. Literally depending on God's boundless supply for their survival, it is doubtful that they were ever worried about losing a sock at the local Laundromat.

Reminded again how much we need reminding, I recalled the words framed on that church wall. The subject of that masterpiece was *El Shaddai*—God All Sufficient . . . *Jehovah-Jireh*—The Lord Provider. No matter how artfully the names were arranged, the message was clear: whatever you need, whatever you lack—I AM! And as that message came into sharp focus, I felt compelled once more to compose a few reminders of my own.

I AM the Maker of the Heavens

I AM the Bright and Morning Star

I AM the Breath of All Creation

Who always was

And is to come

As I scribbled down phrases that described God's infinity, the words became a mirror reflecting just how insignificant we are without him. It is a truth each of us chooses to forget, that is, until we find ourselves face-to-face with that wall of limitations, emblazoned with our one-word definition—*wanting*.

Before life ratchets up that far, remember Belshazzar; a king who actually believed in all the fancy names bestowed on him. Lacking nothing but humility, this arrogant Babylonian ruler spent his time throwing extravagant banquets to show off the wealth he had managed to squirrel away. The king's grandeur was beyond all words; that is, until it was described in writing . . . on a wall.

Belshazzar's bragging days were brought to an abrupt end when his most outrageous banquet was interrupted by a party crasher. The intruder was *El Shaddai* himself; the one real treasure the king had never bothered to acquire—or even acknowledge. But the uninvited visitor was familiar with the king, and proceeded to publicly describe the man, in writing.

As the hall of drunken partyers froze in fear, the very finger of God scribbled a message into the palace plaster. No matter where you stood in the large room, the profound exhibit had the ability to catch your eye. The etching was a masterpiece of simplicity, and it boiled Belshazzar's hoarding, God-ignoring existence down to a single word. "You have been weighed on the scales and found *wanting*" (Daniel 5:27).

Suffice it to say it was a definition he couldn't live with; a handwritten reminder of human nature none of us can afford to ignore.

From the meeting hall of my youth department those years ago, to the concert halls of today, I have encountered more than a few defining moments. Every word and wall I've faced has had the ability to confine me to my limitations, or remind me of my unlimited access to the ultimate definition.

∽

I AM the Spirit deep inside you

I AM the Word upon your heart

I AM the One who even knew you

Before your birth

Before you were

∽

When we deliberately confront our squirrelly nature and consciously try to get a better mental picture of who God is to us, we each inevitably add another description of him to the church wall.

I AM the Fount of Living Water

The Risen Son of Man

The Healer of the Broken

Every time we consider one of God's facets and call upon his name, every time we involve him in our troubles and include him in our triumphs, we illustrate—with our very lives—another dimension of his character. And in the process we expand the limitations of our own frame.

I AM your Savior and Redeemer

Who bore the sins of man

The Author and Perfecter

Beginning and the End

I AM

Knowing that life can be interrupted at any time by the handwriting on the wall, I choose to keep a snapshot of my nutty behavior in the back of my mind, and a mental picture of that masterpiece poster in the forefront of my thoughts. The winter of the unknown is always approaching, and the names of God are an ever-present collection of answers to whatever questions arise—whether they are posed by a kid in class or Einstein.

Before the Earth—I AM

The Universe—I AM

In every heart—I AM

Oh, where you are—I AM

The Lord of Love—I AM

The King of Kings—I AM

The Holy Lamb—I AM

Above all things

It's true that God's abundance can never be fully described, (no matter how many adjectives we use). And yes, all of humanity can be summed up with a single word—*wanting*. But if you remind yourself daily that you constantly need reminding, you'll never have to scrape the bottom of the barrel; for the great I AM is enough and then some. He is ever ready to supply whatever you need—everything from socks to snacks.

⚜ PRAYER ⚜

When I am faced with walls that confine me, let me never forget that among your many names you called yourself—the Door.

"Moses said to God, 'Suppose I go to the Israelites and say to them, "The God of your fathers has sent me to you," and they ask me, "What is his name?" Then what shall I tell them?'

God said to Moses, 'I Am who I Am. This is what you are to say to the Israelites. I Am has sent me to you.'"

EXODUS 3:13, 14

I AM

♯ BY MARK SCHULTZ ♯

I AM the Maker of the Heavens
I AM the Bright and Morning Star
I Am the Breath of All Creation
Who always was
And is to come

I AM the One who walked on water
I AM the One who calmed the seas
I AM the Miracles and Wonders
So come and see
Follow me and you will know

Chorus:
I AM the Fount of Living Water
The Risen Son of Man
The Healer of the Broken
And when you cry
I AM your Savior and Redeemer
Who bore the sins of man
The Author and Perfecter
Beginning and the End
I AM

I AM the Spirit deep inside you
I AM the Word upon your heart
I AM the One who even knew you
Before your birth
Before you were

Bridge:
Before the Earth (I AM)
The Universe (I AM)
In every heart (I AM)
Oh, where you are (I AM)
The Lord of Love (I AM)
The King of Kings (I AM)
The Holy Lamb (I AM)
Above all things

Ken Steorts

The founding guitarist of the Christian rock band Skillet, Ken Steorts formed the band with lead singer and bassist John Cooper and drummer Trey McClurkin. The trio debuted in 1996 with a self-titled LP. Ken left the band in 1999 to build Visible School, a discipleship-based music college in Memphis, Tennessee, for worship leaders, technicians, music business professionals, and ministry bands (www.visibleschool.com).

After having spent years leading and training worship teams and bands, earning a Master of Music in Composition and BFA in Commercial Music—Recording Technology at the University of Memphis, touring as a Dove Award–nominated songwriter/musician, and working in management as well as marketing within the music industry, Ken is currently pursuing his doctorate in Sociological Research at Oxford Graduate School.

Ken also directs Visible Media Group, which facilitates and supports local and national music groups in the modern church, introducing them to the mainstream media through concert promotion, artist development, and internet marketing. Ken's three-piece modern rock band, the beep, plays shows regionally and releases indie projects.

Ken is happily married to his wife, Joy, and they have two sons, Freedman and Skye.

Blind Faith

The sun was going down. The stars were coming out, and I didn't have to check my watch to know I was late. But everything was under control, and it was about time.

A few months back nothing was going right; lost my job, lost my girl, and was considering grabbing my camping gear and getting lost myself. But I kept my head, got on my knees, and remembered to make God part of the solution.

Now I was working two jobs. I was back in school, and started going to a new church. The young people there made me feel at home. Being a musician, I even joined their band.

Nights and weekends we ministered to youth all over the area; a concert/Bible study kind of thing. The theme this week was "faith and the ongoing purposes of God." And though the sun was going down and I was running late, I wasn't concerned; everything in my life was looking up.

Stopping at a red light, I gazed up at the night sky and marveled. God planned the placement of every star, every planet—right down to the rings around Saturn—and that same all-knowing God has plans for me.

As I sat blissfully behind the wheel, waiting for the light to turn, a sudden, unexpected light switched on inside of me. *Wait a second! Saturn has rings? How do I know that's true?* Squinting back up at the stars, I pondered, *Can't see them with the naked eye. Why do I believe they exist? Because a fifth grade science book said it was so? Because NASA scientists agree?*

That's when it hit me. Most of us will never bother to view Saturn's rings. We believe what the experts say and have no need for confirmation, even though high-powered telescopes abound. Oh! To have *that* kind of trust in God—that you don't have to see him to *know* he's there.

It was one of those eureka moments that had me scrounging for a pencil and a scrap of paper. In a flash I was scribbling down a collection of words that wouldn't stop.

I ask him, "When will I be free?"

He said, "I am."

Asking him, "When will I change?"

He said, "No matter now, no matter now."

I was amazed by the words. Every scrawled syllable was about trust—going both ways. Every line was an acknowledgment of a dependence on a power I could not see.

The bliss I had felt moments before was now turning to tears. The light changed and I found myself scribbling on the steering wheel as I drove. It was exhilarating and dangerous. But I figured if I was writing about blind faith, I might as well practice it.

Saturn has a ring around it

You can never see it with your eyes

Saturn has a ring around it

Many moons know this to be true

As I parked my van in the driveway, I could hear the Bible study group inside; the meeting was well underway. Still, I continued to write furiously. Turning the scrap of paper over, the pencil continued to move.

Heaven has a ring around it

The angels sing a song over you

Heaven has a ring around you

If you don't see it, know that it's true

As I finished and the realization of what I had written settled over me, I couldn't hold back the tears. It dawned on me that I truly believed, though I had never seen. Eventually, realizing I was late, I wiped my face and decided to join my friends. As I crossed the threshold, the group was nearing the end of their discussion on faith. But that night I didn't need to see the word on a blackboard to know I had it.

Two years later, as my band, Skillet, was finishing our first record, we realized we needed one more song. We had exhausted eighteen cuts searching, when I considered offering "Saturn." Finally, when no one else spoke up, I began to strum the intro. I got through a verse and a chorus before the producers stopped me. They didn't have to hear it all to know they'd found it.

Not long after that, on another night, as the stars were coming out, a young Minneapolis girl sat on her dorm room floor, sobbing. For her it was almost too late. Everything was out of control. Like me, she thought she had lost everything. In fact, sitting there, she was debating the pros and cons of ending her life. As far as she could see, no one cared about her enough to make plans. Then a voice from her radio interrupted the debate.

You ask him, "How can you be real?"

He said, "You'll be."

Knowing him how you do

Now he says, "Rest in this, rest in this."

For her it was a life-changing, life-saving eureka moment that required no confirmation. In an instant, everything was under control.

"Saturn" never went to No. 1 on the charts, because some radio stations "didn't get it." That's fine. Some of us never do. We go to work, drive our cars, attend Bible studies, listen to our radios and never really get that God planned the placement of every star, every planet—right down to the rings around Saturn. And that same all-knowing God has a plan for us all.

To "get" that divine plan is simple, really. All we have to do is trust God's Word as easily, as matter-of-factly, as we do a science book description of a planet we know exists, but never bother to confirm by telescope.

Heaven has a ring around you

If you don't see it, know that it's true

Help me to make your plans, my plans; your solutions, the answers to all my problems. Let my faith in you be as strong when my eyes are open, as it is when they are closed. And though I do not see your hand, let me feel it holding mine; guiding, directing, every day.

"Thomas said to him, 'My Lord and my God!'

Then Jesus told him, 'Because you have seen me, you have believed; blessed are those who have not seen and yet have believed.'"

JOHN 20:28, 29

Saturn

⟩ WORDS AND MUSIC BY KEN STEORTS ⟨

I ask him, "When will I be free?"
He said, "I am."
Asking him, "When will I change?"
He said, "No matter now, no matter now."

Chorus:
Saturn has a ring around it
You can never see it with your eyes
Saturn has a ring around it
Many moons know this to be true

You ask him, "How can you be real?"
He said, "You'll be."
Knowing him how you do
Now he says, "Rest in this, rest in this."

Heaven has a ring around it
The angels sing a song over you
Heaven has a ring around you
If you don't see it know that it's true

Marty Funderburk

Marty Funderburk's dream of a career in music began on his family's farm in rural Mississippi. With every intention of becoming a high school band director, he studied Music Education at Mississippi State University until suddenly he felt a higher calling to pursue a career in Christian music. This led him to Nashville, where he completed degrees in Biblical Studies and Church Music at a Christian college in the heart of Music City. Following graduation, he toured for six years with Life Action Ministries as a part of a nationwide revival team.

In 1987, Marty returned to Nashville to work within the Christian music industry. After finding success as a studio singer he formed the group Beyond the Blue with his friends

Steve Smith and Richard Kelly, and the trio was met with al-most immediate success, signing with Word Records.

Marty returned to his southern roots after touring with Beyond the Blue and is now a producer and songwriter for Daywind. His writing credits include the No. 1 song, "Forever Changed" performed by The Kingdom Heirs, and "Love Came Gently" featured on CMT's "A Skaggs Family Christmas" and "Top 20 Countdown." He received two Dove Award nomina-tions (Southern Gospel Song of the Year and Blue Grass Song of the Year) at the 2006 GMA Awards.

The Travel Brochure

Sheet music—it's just a couple of folded pages stapled together. But to a lonely boy growing up in 1960s rural Mississippi, those sheets of musical notes were the lines and dots of a map; a travel brochure, capable of taking me anywhere my imagination wanted to go. And the vehicle for that journey was my parents' old upright piano.

Sitting for hours at that keyboard, trying to duplicate the gospel songs I heard my mother play, I'd glance up at the sheet music displayed at nose level and stare at the costumed quartets pictured on the covers. Day after day, as my fingers fumbled to recreate those stirring melodies, I'd look up at the face of Jake Hess, marvel at his style, and dream of joining him and The Statesmen on their travels.

Eventually, that imagined musical journey became so much a part of my nightly prayers and daily routine that I managed to get that old upright piano to actually, physically move! (My parents rolled it into my bedroom—for their own sanity's sake.)

As the years passed and my exploration of music matured, I learned to navigate my way around a song. By high school I was drafting my own melodic charts of lines and dots. And within a year of graduation those musical maps became so stirring, so imaginative that I found myself actually, physically moving—to Nashville; the place where musical dreams come true.

The big city was amazing. Although it resembled the destination I had envisioned sitting at the ol' upright, it was more than I expected. To a kid who grew up on a spacious, uneventful farm, the place was loud, bustling, and unbelievably crowded. And it didn't take long for me to discover that so was the Nashville music scene.

The sidewalks of Music Row were nothing like the dirt paths back home. They were jammed with songwriters and performers from all over the country. Everywhere I looked I saw young hopefuls carrying guitars and demo tapes. Each one had a look of confidence, expectation; as if they knew, beyond all doubt, that their face would one day grace the cover of their own sheet music. To say the sight was intimidating would be an understatement.

How could I possibly compete? Here I was just a farm boy fresh off the turnip truck; just another face in a very loud crowd. All I had was a suitcase stuffed with clothes and a head filled with dreams sparked by those folded, stapled travel brochures I once studied at nose level.

That first year I felt more alone in the middle of the city than I ever did back in rural Mississippi. My only companion was the smiling face of Jake Hess, urging me not to turn around. Somehow I knew that though the road behind me was a dirt path, the road ahead was paved with wonders.

The first positive sign along that road was my timing. I had arrived in Nashville just as gospel was finally reaching the ears of music lovers outside the church. Songs like "Oh Happy Day" were getting airplay on the radio. A wide range of gospel artists were starting to show up on TV; performers from Amy Grant to The Statesmen Quartet were fast becoming recognizable faces and household names.

Suddenly all those years sitting at the family piano began to pay off. I signed my first writing contract and quickly began churning out songs that reflected the childlike faith of my nightly prayers.

In no time I landed my first record deal and started touring with a group whose name reflected my seemingly limitless bounds—Beyond the Blue. I was finally on the road, living the life I had dreamed about when I stared at those old quartet pictures.

That road took me to places I never imagined on the farm. Playing on stages nationwide, I experienced the thrill of performing before countless live audiences. Traveling across the country, I reveled in the energy that flows between performers and their fans. But nothing I experienced compared with seeing the crowd's reaction to the gospel message in my songs. There's something life-fulfilling about watching the face of an individual who just got a glimpse of the ultimate travel brochure.

Living on the road, traveling in the fast lane, was definitely a trip. But as I watched the world pass by my bus window, I realized that it didn't compare to the ride of seeing a searching soul connect to my musical map of lines and dots.

When that notion hit me, I found myself at a crossroads.

Which way do I go? Was the family piano truly the vehicle that launched my career as a musician? Or, had the ol' upright been more of a tool, shaping my true vocation? Was the best place for me on the road? Or was I just spinning my wheels?

You can't pick a direction until you know where you are. And you'll never make that connection until you discover not only who you are, but who is guiding you. When that insight finally hit home, it actually, physically moved me.

I realized that my place was not on the road, but rather at a piano charting the path, mapping out the Way. And my journey to this discovery was not just the result of a childhood dream, but rather the gentle directing hand of the one who had been the subject of all my songs.

Every step of the way, even when I felt I was walking alone, my unseen collaborator was close by. He is the one who put the dream in my heart and the talent in my hand, who urged me to become what I'd always been—a composer of sheet music, a songwriter.

Discovering my true vocation eventually led me to the most amazing destination. I began writing, composing with the energy of a child and the insight of seasoned traveler. And seemingly overnight those charts of lines and dots were picked up and recorded by some of gospel's finest artists: "The Cross Said It All" with Kim Hopper, "If Not for the Old Rugged Cross" with LordSong, "No Stranger to the Valley" with Mike Bowling, and "Love Came Gently" with Ricky Skaggs and Sharon White.

Yet with all my success there was still one childhood dream outstanding—being a part of the Statesmen Quartet. But by now that goal was just wishful thinking; most of the figures of that legendary generation had either retired or passed on. I figured that if our paths had been meant to cross, they would have done so by now.

Then one day I switched on the TV and Bill Gaither appeared—a fellow who's written a few songs. Surrounding him were a number of faces I recognized from the sheet music Mom once displayed on the ol' upright. The program was part of the successful *Homecoming* series, which was once more introducing gospel to the ears and the eyes of music lovers, both inside and outside the church.

Watching and listening to those old-timers harmonize was a trip. It took me back, all the way back to Mississippi, back to my folks' rural farm. And as I sat glued to the screen, mesmerized by it all, a smile I didn't expect caught my eye. It was Jake Hess! He was still spry, still singing, still riveting audiences with that unmistakable flare. And as I watched him work the crowd, I got to thinking—there may still be a chance for my dream.

Then, in the middle of a writing session, my partner Daryl Williams turned to me and out of the blue announced, "Jake Hess is looking for songs for a new project." That startling collection of unexpected words actually, physically moved me to the piano.

Sitting down at the keyboard I began to reminisce about my childhood hero; about his life, his long journey, and mine.

I'm a worn and weary traveler

I have walked so many miles

Though the path is long and winding

The Lord has been there all the while

I thought about the road and how it had no doubt taken him to places he never imagined. I envisioned the countless stages he had stood on, and how he must have reveled in the energy that flowed between him and the tens of thousands that heard him sing.

The road has led me on a journey

Distant lands so far from home

But I've had no cause for fear

My Lord is always near

I have never walked alone

Although my fingers fumbled to find just the right chords, it was easy to understand why Jake Hess had spent his life on the road. Like me, he had found his vocation; he knew that communicating the gospel through song was what he did best. Nothing else could compare. Nothing else was as life-fulfilling as pointing to the one who had been the subject of all his songs.

I have never walked alone

I have held the unseen hand

He will lead me safely home

To the shores of Beulah Land

No sooner had Daryl and I finished the song than we heard that Jake's health was declining. We rushed the sheet music to his producer, Roger Talley, and waited. Eventually, after a little nail biting, we received word that the smiling face I used to study at nose level loved it. "I Have Never Walked Alone" would be a cut on a Jake Hess album.

But just as that gospel veteran was preparing to record the tune, he fell ill. Although we hoped for the best, it seemed unlikely that Jake would ever grace the stage again, much less enter a studio and finish his album. But then, the unbelievable happened.

It was as if something within the singer urged him not to turn around. Although far from well, the old Statesman somehow found the determination to acknowledge the dirt path one last time—that earthly road he had traveled so long.

Though I've had to walk by faith

Through it all, I've always known

I'm walking with a friend

Who will be there to the end

I have never walked alone

The song became the first release off the album. And what a thrill it was to hear my childhood hero singing a song I had written just for him.

Now the journey's almost over

My time on earth will reach an end

I reminisce about this good life

And all the places I have been

The single was a hit. But as the chorus began to reverberate over the nation's airwaves, the gospel legend himself finally, spiritually, moved—stepping off his dirt path onto those wondrous streets paved with gold.

On the day of Jake Hess's funeral, a friend called me from the ceremony. She said she was holding a folded piece of paper displaying Jake's picture. As she described the funeral program it was reminiscent of sheet music, right down to the lyrics of a single song. She read them to me, and it was as if the words were printed as a deliberate comfort to his family and fans. Of all the hundreds of classics Jake will be remembered for singing, I was amazed at the lyrics chosen to sum up his long, well-lived life—"I Have Never Walked Alone."

The smiling face of Jake Hess had been on the sheet music, the musical chart that directed me to my vocation. And my sheet music had been his travel brochure, pointing him toward his ultimate journey. Every step of the way, though we never met, our mutual unseen collaborator had guided our paths, for he was the subject of all our songs.

There's a better home awaiting

So remember when I'm gone

I'll be in that promised land

Where I'll see those nail-scarred hands

And I'll never walk alone

One day when I make that ultimate move, it won't matter how big the City is, I won't need a map to find Jake Hess. I'll just start singing about how "I have never walked alone," and his familiar voice will chime in. A certain quartet will show up and split the melody into parts, and a mass choir of family and friends will take the up the chorus. Everyone will compose his own verse about the journey, and sing about the unseen hand that led the way home. For there, we'll *all* be songwriters, with no more need of sheet music, or travel brochures.

 Prayer

Though I know a man's gift makes room for him and brings him before the great (Proverbs 18:16), let me never forget that you supply the gift and guide the way.

> "And surely I am with you always, to the very end of the age."
>
> MATTHEW 28:20

I Have Never Walked Alone

WORDS AND MUSIC BY MARTY FUNDERBURK AND DARYL WILLIAMS

I'm a worn and weary traveler
I have walked so many miles
Though the path is long and winding
The Lord has been there
    all the while
The road has led me on a journey
Distant lands so far from home
But I've had no cause for fear
My Lord is always near
I have never walked alone

Chorus:
I have never walked alone
I have held the unseen hand
He will lead me safely home
To the shores of Beulah Land
Though I've had to walk by faith
Through it all, I've always known
I'm walking with a friend
Who will be there to the end
I have never walked alone

Now the journey's almost over
My time on earth will reach an end
I reminisce about this good life
And all the places I have been
But there's a better home awaiting
So remember when I'm gone
I'll be in that promised land
Where I'll see those
    nail-scarred hands
I will never walk alone

Michael Peterson

Michael Peterson was born in Tucson, Arizona, in 1959, and grew up in Richland, Washington. His love of music was developed through spending time with his grandmother, who encouraged his interests in singing, songwriting, and playing guitar.

Though his music career actually began in the 80s (his first release, a self-titled collection of contemporary Christian songs, came out on Sparrow Records in 1986), it was the success of the hit country single, "Drink, Swear, Steal and Lie" that catapulted Michael Peterson into the national spotlight in 1997. His follow-up release, "From Here to Eternity," earned the singer his first No. 1 hit. His debut disc was certified gold and Peterson was recognized as country music's top-selling new male artist of 1997 and 1998. With the release of his second album, *Being Human*, he also won the 1999 Male Star of Tomorrow Award at the TNN/ Music City News Awards.

Michael released the single "Modern Man" on his new label, Monument, in 2002. Though a shake-up at the Sony label sidetracked his career for a couple years, in 2004 AGR/Universal acquired the rights to his latest album and released it in Europe to great success. Michael's European concerts have since received rave reviews, and he has also performed for the U.S. Armed Forces, even traveling to Iraq to encourage the troops. The release of his newest CD is eagerly awaited both in Europe and the U.S.

MICHAEL PETERSON

Small Things

A snowflake fell from the sky and melted into a river bound for a Canadian dam. Winding through the spillway, the accumulation of melted snow roared over the turbines and generated just enough electricity to turn a Toronto traffic light red; thereby prompting my taxi to stop at the intersection.

I drummed my fingers on my guitar case impatiently. I was cold. I wanted nothing more than to get to my hotel room, grab a hot meal, and rest up for my appearance the next morning on a local TV talk show.

But as the cab idled at the corner, waiting for the light to change, my eye caught something brown amid all the winter white. Through my frosted window, I saw that across the street on the sidewalk lay a man wrapped up like a frozen burrito in a blanket of cardboard. He had no shoes.

Gazing at the shivering soul, I felt for him. What could I possibly do to help? But just as my mind began to turn, so did the traffic light. And as the taxi drove away, I watched the image of the man's bare feet disappear into a white curtain of falling snow.

The next morning a switch was flipped in a TV studio, generating just enough electricity to illuminate my dressing room. As I pulled my guitar from its case and started warming up for my performance, the studio's janitor appeared in my doorway. I guess he liked what he heard. He was a friendly fellow. And as I strummed the guitar, we struck up a conversation.

"Yeah, you think flying from Tennessee to Canada is a trip? Every morning I ride my bike to work. And it's not easy, especially this time of year. But after what I saw this morning, I'm not about to complain. On the way here I rode past a man lying on the sidewalk, shivering. He was rolled up in some cardboard."

My strumming fingers stopped cold.

"The poor guy was actually barefooted. There was a store nearby, so I stopped and got him some socks and a pair of shoes." The janitor shrugged his shoulders, "It was the least I could do."

I was stunned, speechless. Yet before my face could register my amazement, a young man wearing headphones stuck his head around the door and motioned to me with his clipboard. "Mr. Peterson, you're up next. Follow me."

Nodding to the janitor, I picked up my guitar and followed the floor director down a hallway in a slow, surreal daze. All I could see was the image of the barefoot man, wrapped in cardboard, disappearing into the blizzard of snow. All I could hear were the janitor's words: "It was the least I could do."

I was brought back to the moment by the studio's bright lights and a voice reverberating over the house speakers. It was the guest just preceding me—the head of Social Services for eastern Ontario. She was winding up her segment with a classic story about the greatest helping hand of our age, Mother Teresa.

"Once, she was asked how she had managed to do so many great things with her life. And in her typical, humble way, Mother Teresa replied, 'We can do no great things—only small things with great love.'"

It was as if someone flipped a switch, generating just enough wisdom to illuminate my path. Those words, coming just moments after hearing the janitor's tale, set my mind to turning again. The smallest good deed is better than the grandest of intentions. The notion was profound, earth-shaking, yet as simple and transforming as a reassuring smile.

That barefoot man may have been exposed to the elements, but when I drove away, I was the one left out in the cold. Sitting in that taxi, I tried to conjure up some grand gesture that might help the homeless fellow. But I was so busy trying to think of something big that the simple combination of warm caring hands and woolen socks never occurred to me.

It is amazing how much good a little good can do. It is a listening ear, a gentle touch, a single act of kindness along a roadside. It's going out of your way to help someone you may never meet again. It's a moment, a drop of water, a single snowflake melting into the river of life, spinning that generator of love, which lights the world.

There's a dam out on the river

Holding back a wealth of water deep and wide

It rushes through the channels

And turns the turbines

It puts power in the wires

That wind their way across the hills into my town

Down the street into these houses

Without a sound

Had I chosen a different taxi at the airport, I would have missed that traffic light. I never would have seen that man's bare feet, or felt the poignancy of Mother Teresa's words. And the janitor's small selfless deed would never have been recorded on these pages.

We all know some human angels

At times it seems the work they do is all in vain

Just a few tears of compassion on a world in flames

But the tears all come together

And a river starts to flow

And out there in the darkness

A light begins to glow

It's the little things that create transformation. Seconds create minutes, minutes create hours. Yet it is in those split seconds of time, it is in those little everyday life choices where big changes are made.

In a moment, a European farm girl bowed, took the name Teresa, and became the mother of India's outcasts. In an instant, a Toronto janitor became a sidewalk custodian, kneeling in the snow with a pair of shoes for a discarded soul. And in a flash of illumination that forever changed the way we all should see ourselves, Jesus knelt before his followers, removed their sandals and washed their feet.

We can do no great thing alone

We can only do small things with great love

The truth is all of us are helpless without Heaven above

Giving us strength to do small things with great love

If a flake of snow can fall from the sky, join with other crystals, and create a blizzard to make a man shiver, and if a similar snowflake can melt into a river and become a mighty current capable of lighting a city, then one small gesture from each of us can change the temperature of our world and generate enough light that all might see the power of small things.

Sitting in my seat waiting for the plane to taxi to the gate, I stared at the seatbelt light and drummed my fingers on my guitar case impatiently. I wanted nothing more than to get home and embrace Tacey and our daughters, Amanda and Lauren. It had been just a little trip, across the Canada–U.S. border and back. But coming out of the cold I had returned with a transforming idea, one I'm sure my girls would consider huge.

If Jesus showed his great love by simply washing the feet of his followers, surely, when I get home I can rinse out a few dishes.

Now, heaven knows

I've been in need a time or two

So I won't underestimate the good

A little good can do

✑ PRAYER ✒

Let me never get so busy with the big screen movie of my life that I fail to notice the little moments. For if you are the main character of my story, the devil's not in the details . . . you are.

> 66 When he had finished washing their feet, he put on his clothes and returned to his place. . . . 'I have set you an example that you should do as I have done for you.' 99
>
> JOHN 13:12, 15

Great Love

{ BY MICHAEL PETERSON AND CRAIG WISEMAN }

There's a dam out on the river
Holding back a wealth of
　water deep and wide
It rushes through the channels
And turns the turbines

It puts power in the wires
That wind their way across the hills
　into my town
Down the street into these houses
Without a sound

We can do no great thing alone
We can only do small things with
　great love
The truth is all of us are helpless
　without Heaven above
Giving us strength to do small
　things with great love

We all know some human angels
At times it seems the work they do
　is all in vain
Just a few tears of compassion on a
　world in flames

But the tears all come together
And a river starts to flow
And out there in the darkness
A light begins to glow

Now, heaven knows
I've been in need a time or two
So I won't underestimate the good
A little good can do

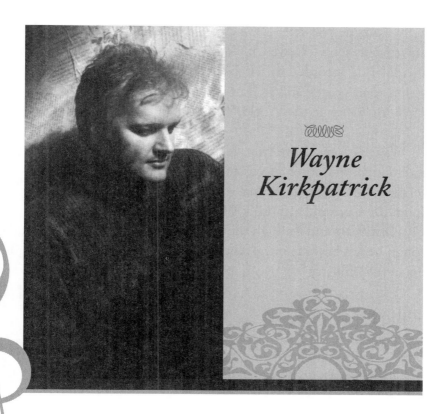

Wayne Kirkpatrick

Wayne Kirkpatrick has been writing songs since the age of fourteen. After a trip to Bible camp, where he learned how to play "Just a Closer Walk with Thee" on guitar, Wayne's path took a momentous turn toward a life of music. In those early years, Wayne often tried out his lyrics on his pastor father's congregation. It was clear then that he had gift for expressing himself through song—a gift that would serve him well when he later met his high school sweetheart (and future wife), Fran.

Wayne moved to Nashville to attend college, and his brother Karey followed suit. In the course of working on a project, Karey managed to get a tape of Wayne's music to Amy Grant's manager, Michael Blanton. Before long, Wayne's first record with

Billy Sprague was cut—"What a Way to Go." Other records and success soon followed, including hit songs such as "Place in this World," recorded by Michael W. Smith, world tours, television appearances, and a Grammy "Song of the Year" Award in 1996 for "Change the World," recorded by Eric Clapton.

Wayne's songs have been recorded by such artists as those mentioned and other successful country, gospel, and pop performers including Martina McBride, Babyface, Wynonna Judd, Joe Cocker, Faith Hill, Bonnie Raitt, and Garth Brooks. Over the years and through the recording of some two hundred songs, he has become one of the most well-respected songwriters in the industry.

WAYNE KIRKPATRICK

Human Beings . . . Becoming

I love to explore the past. History fascinates me; by using the 360 degrees of 20/20 hindsight, we mortals can actually come close to seeing ourselves the way God sees us—objectively.

Requiring only the desire to do so, we are able to step back and view the big picture of time. Examining people and events from that godlike perspective enables us to connect the truth we know today with what transpired back then. Such unbiased exploration looks beneath the surface, past the prejudice of the era, allowing the actions of the most infamous man to be understood in full, and maybe even forgiven.

Viewing all sides of an event without discrimination is a gift, an asset of our human nature. It is an attribute that helps us mortals do more than merely exist. That godlike view helps us to grow, to mature; to be less like human beings, and more like humans . . . becoming. But looking back at mankind's long history of war and confrontation, it is obvious that this viewpoint has rarely been in focus.

The best modern example I've found of willful objectivity is the work of documentary director Ken Burns. Perusing the past through the lens of his neutral camera, Burns transports his viewers into the hearts and minds of every character on both sides of the conflict. His films are the closest I've seen to that godlike view. And the most vivid of these efforts is his PBS masterpiece, *The Civil War*.

Being the history buff that I am, that epic riveted me to the screen. Watching as the two sides of an angry nation dug in their heels, I saw countless occasions when compromise was possible but repeatedly thwarted; blocked by the closed-minded natures of a stubborn few. Tempers mounted, fists clenched, and lines were eventually drawn.

Through Ken Burns's eyes I easily saw the South's point of view and understood the North's position. But what I couldn't comprehend was why the two sides of this divided house willingly chose to close their eyes to each other's view. If only they could have seen themselves from the perspective I was using. But with their eyes shut tight, each side crossed the line. And over half a million died.

As I sat, eyes glued to this visual history lesson, I saw a collection of words fade in on the screen. White on black—much like the Civil War itself. The words hung there for a moment, marking the end of one segment and the beginning of another—BETTER ANGELS OF OUR NATURE.

The silent phrase spoke volumes. The musician in me woke up. *Better angels*. It was lyrical. *Of our nature*. Simple. Profound. I wrote it down.

As the documentary continued, I discovered that those five words had been spoken by President Abraham Lincoln at his second inaugural. It was a phrase he borrowed from Shakespeare to describe what his war-torn nation needed to focus on most; the other side's point of view—"With malice toward none, with charity for all."

Everyone that heard his words that day had also heard the sound of cannons. Each listener, gathered around him on the Capitol steps, had also gathered around the graves of family and friends who had died at the hands of family and friends. It was not a forgiving crowd. And as I watched, I realized that what I was viewing was not just human history, but timeless human nature.

He fell to his knees and he cried out for mercy

Heartfelt confessionals to an angry mob

But vengeance was theirs

As they bellowed for justice

"Death to the man who has sinned against God."

Given the blood, destruction, raids, and retaliations of those four years of war, I found it hard to imagine that anyone could let the stone drop from their hands.

I joined in the chant, feeling so high and mighty

Pointing a finger from up on my throne

'Til I looked in his tears and I caught my reflection

And I knew that I could not cast the first stone

Standing at that podium, Lincoln stood his ground, transformed. No longer was he a human being concerned with his political future; at that moment he was a human becoming far more than his humble history predicted. Illuminated by Shakespeare's five little words, Lincoln searched himself. That unbiased examination helped him take a step back and see things from God's objective point of view. And looking beyond the prejudice of the era, past the cries for retribution, he focused on reconciliation.

Using the 360 degrees of 20/20 hindsight, the president connected the truth of what had to begin that day with the tragedy of all that had transpired. And calling on his countrymen to seek out the better angels of their own natures, he reminded them of their godlike ability to take a step back, understand the big picture, and even forgive.

Let the gavel fall slowly tho' truth's been revealed

Sequester the jury for a moment to feel

And in the courts of compassion

I hope we can appeal

To the better angels of our nature

The choice of *better angels* implies that a less than good nature is always vying to control us. Like the struggle between the North and South, the tug-of-war between our two-sided characters is violent, draining, and seemingly unending.

Day after day, we are so busy being human—clenching our fists and drawing lines between us and them—that we can't see the division within ourselves. We bang the gavel, cast the first stone, and wonder why the world around us is no longer civil.

I think Lincoln realized that his world, as a whole, had no chance unless the individuals living in it chose to change. He made that deliberate choice to heed the better angels of his nature, and urged his divided nation to do likewise.

Angels of mercy—angels of light

Angels of darkness—angels of might

Angels with voices that whisper so clear

Who do I lean to? Who do I hear?

I love to explore the past, especially my own. Back on that historic day so long ago, as I watched Ken Burns's masterpiece, Shakespeare's phrase gave me more than a song. When those five little words appeared on the screen, I came close to seeing myself the way God sees me: I am a human, not just being, but constantly becoming. If I want my world, my future, to change for the better, I have to make that same choice—every day. And all it requires is the desire to do so.

Better angels of our nature. The words hung there for a moment, marking the end of one segment of my life and the beginning of another.

∽ PRAYER ∽

Let me not get so busy just being that I forget to step back, look at my world, and see what you want me to become.

> "The Lord does not look at the things man looks at. Man looks at the outward appearance, but the Lord looks at the heart."

1 SAMUEL 16:7

Better Angels
of Our Nature

⸙ WORDS AND MUSIC BY WAYNE KIRKPATRICK ⸙

He fell to his knees and he cried out
for mercy
Heartfelt confessionals to an angry mob
But vengeance was theirs
As they bellowed for justice
"Death to the man who has sinned
against God."

I joined in the chant, feeling so high
and mighty
Pointing a finger from up on my throne
'Til I looked in his tears and I caught
my reflection
And I knew that I could not cast the
first stone

Let the gavel fall slowly tho' truth's been
revealed
Sequester the jury for a moment to feel
And in the courts of compassion
I hope we can appeal
To the better angels of our nature
To the better angels of our nature

I walked along on my soft streets
of plenty
She walked the alleys of anguish
and need
While clutching my greed I was struck
by a vision
But for the grace of God, that could
be me

And we gather in chambers of lofty
ideals
Still debating the giving when handed
the bill
But in the congress of kindness
I hope that we can yield
To the better angels of our nature
To the better angels of our nature

Angels of mercy—angels of light
Angels of darkness—angels of might
Angels with voices that whisper so clear
Who do I lean to? Who do I hear?

We are building our world with a
fevered emotion
While trying to keep it from
coming apart
But as we reach for the dream
Can we still reach within us
We won't have the hope if we don't have
the heart

'Cause we're tossed in the gale of a
moral decline
As we drink from the grail of
society's wine
But at humanity's table I hope we
choose to dine
With the better angels of our nature
With the better angels of our nature

Mike Weaver

Since the formation of the band in their University of Mobile days, Mike Weaver and Big Daddy Weave have experienced both huge successes and major setbacks. But through it all, their motivation and purpose has remained clear—to simply keep doing what God has called them to do.

The band hit the ground running in 2002 with their album *One and Only*, which debuted in SoundScan's Christian Top 5 chart and remained in the top twenty for six weeks. The band was honored at ASCAP's 2003 and 2004 Christian Music Awards and received a Dove Award nomination in 2002 for New Artist of the Year.

The group was all set to work on their third project, *What I Was Made For* (Fervent Records, 2005), when disaster in the form of Hurricane Ivan struck their hometown of Mobile, Alabama, leveling the Weaver family home and destroying the home office of the band, which the Weaver parents maintained. Thankfully, their parents were not hurt. The band ended up recording the album there in Mobile. From this album has come yet another No. 1 hit for the band, the classic worship song "You're Worthy of My Praise."

Mike and Big Daddy Weave have been continually on the road, keeping a busy tour schedule with other artists such as Rebecca St. James, FFH, Geoff Moore, Todd Agnew, and Exit East. But Mike, who has become an expert at juggling various roles as co-producer, principal songwriter, lead vocalist, and guitarist for the group, managed to find time to meet and marry the "girl of his dreams," Kandice, even in the midst of chaotic times. As he put it, "When Jesus said, I've come to bring you life, and life abundantly, it was like, that's the gamut. It's not just, I come to bring you the good days abundantly, which some people read into that. It's everything," says Mike. "And the biggest picture of that for me was that I ultimately found the girl I was going to marry literally the same time that the hurricane happened that tore apart my parents' home."

Take a Load Off

On an oval track, measured out to test a runner's endurance, I walked. It was part of a lifelong routine; an attempt to keep my health up, my weight down, and my spirit in tune. Each orbit around that track generated not only perspiration but also a measure of inspiration; for as I walked I talked with God.

Although our conversations were not limited to my daily exercise, it was during these solitary strolls that I labored to shed both my excess weight and lingering baggage. Using the track to sweat off some pounds was easy. But letting go of the past was a much harder road.

It began mid-orbit, during the course of one of my disciplined walks. Somewhere along the way my mind began to wander, and in the time it takes to put one foot in front of the other, I watched the familiar curve of the trail vanish! In its place appeared the narrow aisle of an elementary school bus. Suddenly I was no longer a twenty-something member of the band, Big Daddy Weave; instead, I was once again a pudgy second-grader, dreading that long gauntlet-walk from the bus driver's perch to the backseat.

In an unexpected flashback I saw the childhood faces of the future jocks and prom queens of my Florida hometown. Staring back at me from their bus seats, their condescending attitudes were typical of those destined to be the cool kids. As I stood nervously by the bus driver, realizing there were no seats near the front, I could hear the snickering of the gallery commenting on my nerdish, chubby frame. It wasn't a pleasant memory.

I didn't fit in, and I knew it. The replay of it all was still painful. Back then, searching for an empty seat was part obstacle course, part endurance test. And the track was that long, endless corridor between the seats, measured out to test my resolve.

Squeezing myself through that narrow aisle, inching ever deeper into the enemy's territory, I recall bracing myself for the coming onslaught. But instead of the defiance one might expect from adolescence, I was met with total disregard. Eyes shifted, heads turned, and the tropical temperature in the back of the bus plummeted.

It was an intentional freeze-out, and with each fearful step I shivered more. Scanning every row for a vacancy, time itself seemed to slow in the icy atmosphere. Finally, my desperate eyes glimpsed an opening, and gambling what little remained of my pride, I made my move. But the effort was blocked. No matter where I attempted to sit down, a coat or a pile of books subtly appeared to fill the space. There was no rest for the weary.

"Scoot over! Let him in!"

The strong, authoritative voice of the bus driver cut through the tension and echoed down the aisle. From his mirrored perspective it was obvious that I was getting nowhere, and that his intervention was my only hope.

"We're not moving till he's seated." The loud timbre of his declaration was music to my ears. The situation was out of my hands, and I was happy, actually relieved, to let him take control.

"The longer he stands, the longer we sit!" The resonance of his voice, the reason in his words, forced the cool kids to warm up to the idea of me sitting down.

"Scoot!" With his command, a vacancy appeared next to me. Relieved, I took a load off and finally sat down. Immediately, the metallic grinding of the gears vibrated the bus frame, and the wheels began to turn.

Coming back to my twenty-something self, I realized I was still standing on the oval track. The sights, sounds, and feelings I had just experienced seemed so fresh, so real; as if I'd been searching for the bus seat that morning, instead of twenty-odd years ago.

Why was I thinking about all this now? And if that bus was finally able to move forward, what was holding me up?

Standing there, perspiring as if I had run a marathon, I realized it wasn't a few extra pounds that were weighing me down, but rather, baggage I had no idea I was carrying.

Desperate. Grasping with a clenched fist

I try to hold my own life in my own hand

Here I was, a fairly successful Christian songwriter, with a very real relationship with the subject of my songs—God! I was productive, happy, and with the exception of being overweight, I enjoyed a full and fairly balanced life. So why was I standing in the middle of a running track, still waiting for a seat on a bus?

Frustration sets in, thought I had this

Failure is the one thing that I can't stand

I struggled with the question for days. I thought about it, prayed about it—even soaked my carpet with tears over it. Finally, I took my frustration to the man I most trusted and admired, my role model, my best friend—my dad.

Recounting the story of my quest for a seat, Dad patiently listened. Then, after hearing about the bus driver's intervention, my father turned and looked at me, "You gotta give it to God, son. Just gotta let it go."

It was not the answer I expected. I had "given it to God" a bazillion times already!

Seeing the frustration in my face, Dad sprouted a wise smile and added, "Your childhood is the foundation of the man you become."

What did he mean? Was I dealing with my sense of helplessness like a second-grader? Or was I handling things differently this time around?

Give it to God. The advice echoed in my head. The sound of Dad's reply replayed itself over and over, like my haunting childhood memory, and like the Scriptures I learned as a boy: "lay aside every weight . . . which so easily ensnares us." How do you do that? How do you set aside a pain so deeply engrained in the brain that you didn't even know it was there? "And let us run with endurance the race that is set before us" (Hebrews 12:1, *NKJV*). Run with endurance? How am I supposed to do *that* when I can be so easily stopped in my tracks while merely walking?

Let it go. Those reverberating words, the confident timbre in Dad's voice—together, they resonated hope and strength. The combination reminded me of the relief I felt when the bus driver took control.

That's it! *He* was the difference.

I could see it now, as clearly as my unexpected flashback. When there was no rest for the weary, the bus driver intervened—*and I let him.* The pudgy second-grader I once was had simply turned over the problem to the one who had both the authority and the power to get things moving again.

It was so simple. The memory of my younger self's actions were not a burden to be blocked out, but a blessing—a foundational lesson to be cherished. That gauntlet walk was not a memento of my past weaknesses, but a monumental reminder of the strength available to us all, every day.

You remind me that taking care of me

Was never in my job description

Now I'm finding you want to fix it all

You're just waiting for permission

Taking Dad's advice I finally, completely let go, and gave the burden of it all to God. Realizing that the fear of failure is what keeps us standing, frozen in one place, I took a load off . . . and finally sat down.

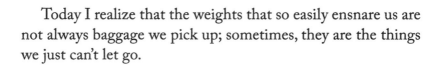

I'm giving up, I'm letting go

Of everything that I've held onto

I'm giving up, I'm letting go

Of everything that I've let hold me

Far too long (for so long) Lord I know

I need to give you full control

Help me give up and let go

Today I realize that the weights that so easily ensnare us are not always baggage we pick up; sometimes, they are the things we just can't let go.

I want to trust you with my whole heart

Not lean on what I think I understand

The longer we stand around and try to handle our problems ourselves, the longer God will sit and wait. It is up to us to surrender to him. He has the authority and the power to get our lives moving. If we let go, lean on his understanding, cast our burdens on him, and sit down, he will give us rest.

And even when I can't see

Jesus, help me still to believe

You're unveiling an unfailing plan

I still walk that oval track to keep my health up and to work on my weight, and along the way I do occasionally flash on that bus ride. But it doesn't bother me anymore. That long ago journey to school is what led to my education.

I've come to realize that God gave us the ability to remember for a reason. It is up to us how we choose to use the gift. Good or bad, our flashbacks are the foundation of the person we become. And despite our weaknesses, we all possess the ability to choose whether our memories haunt us or help us.

Using that runner's track to sweat off the pounds isn't easy. But walking does have a way of putting things into perspective. Each step I take generates not only perspiration but also a measure of inspiration; for as I walk, I talk with God. And the strength I gain from *that* journey makes my every orbit around the sun a little more illuminating . . . and a whole lot lighter.

❧ Prayer ❧

Each day help me to do what is necessary to become more physically fit and spiritually in tune. When I become weary along the way and the baggage of my past seems more than I can carry, illuminate my path with the reassurance of your presence. With each step I take, turn the memory of my weaknesses into a weight-lifting reminder of your strength. And grant me the wisdom to know when to take a stand, when to sit down, when to take a load off, and when to give it to you.

"Come to me, all you who labor and are heavy laden, and I will give you rest."

MATTHEW 11:28 (*NKJV*)

Give Up, Let Go

❧ WORDS AND MUSIC BY MIKE WEAVER ☙

Desperate. Grasping with a
  clenched fist
I try to hold my own life in my
  own hand
Frustration sets in, thought I
  had this
Failure is the one thing that I
  can't stand

Oh, you remind me that taking care
  of me
Was never in my job description
Oh, now I'm finding you want to
  fix it all
You're just waiting for permission

I'm giving up, I'm letting go
Of everything that I've held onto
I'm giving up, I'm letting go
Of everything that I've let hold me
Far too long (for so long)
  Lord I know
I need to give you full control
Help me give up and let go

I want to trust you with my
  whole heart
Not lean on what I think I
  understand
And even when I can't see
Jesus, help me still to believe
You're unveiling an unfailing plan

Oh, but sometimes the old me
  creeps back in
Oh, and the only thing I know to do
  is give it all to you again

Help me give up, help me let go
Help me give up, help me let go
Help me give it all to you

Jason
Roy

Texas-born frontman and guitarist Jason Roy formed the band Building 429 with bassist Scotty Beshears in North Carolina in 2000, borrowing the idea for the band name from a youth group's "429 Challenge," based on Ephesians 4:29. From the beginning the performers (which now also include Jesse Garcia on guitar and keyboard and Michael Anderson on drums) wanted to have a band whose focus would be building others up.

The band got their break through meeting Jason Ingram at a photo shoot, who became a friend to the band. This meeting eventually resulted in a deal with Word Records, and they debuted in 2004 with their *Glory Defined* EP. The title track hit No. 1 on eight different charts and became BMI's 2005 Song of the Year for Christian music. The band also received four

Dove Award nominations and was named the GMA's 2005 New Artist of the Year.

Jason, who has been writing songs for about twelve years now, says the highlight of his career so far was receiving BMI's award for Most Performed Christian Song of the Year for 2004. Since their debut, the band has toured with Casting Crowns, Jeremy Camp, BarlowGirl, and Todd Agnew, among others. Jason has also acted as a spokesperson for the Redeem the Vote campaign (2004).

Jason and his wife, Cortni, reside in Clarksville, Tennessee, with their son, Avery, and their baby daughter, Haven.

In the **Shadow** of the **In-Between**

I was in the middle of nowhere. Above me was a canopy of stars. Below me, a blanket of sand. Somewhere in between I was waiting, listening for the voice of God. But all I heard was the gentle ripple of the tide lapping against the shore.

That sandy sliver of nowhere, just off the North Carolina coast, was my island refuge. Jutting out of the water between the mainland and the vast Atlantic Ocean, it was my outer-bank hideaway; the place where I often retreated when it seemed there were too many options, or too few. No matter what I was trying to find, my search either began or ended on that solitary stretch of sand.

Sunrise on Sunset Beach

Finds me right where I watched it set

Sitting for hours on the western bank of my refuge, I had watched the daylight disappear across the bay, beyond the mainland's hills. The gradual, all-encompassing darkness settled over me like a shroud, reminding me just how little of my world, and my life, I could clearly see. It had been a long dark night of searching. And though the sun was once more beginning to peek over the horizon behind me, I was still in the dark, unsure of which way today's big decision would go.

I spent the night inside myself

But I haven't found me yet

As the sun rose, so did my questions.

"I'm doing what you wanted me to do. But all it has brought me is conflict," I whispered, looking up at the disappearing stars. "Why is that?"

I listened for a reply, but I heard only the sound of water playing against the hull of my beached boat. That little vessel and I had a lot in common. Its wood frame had no doubt been cut from the trunks of deep-rooted trees. Its buoyancy had been tested, and its form fashioned into a vehicle capable of bringing land and water together.

Like my little boat, I too had been severed from my roots and tested for buoyancy.

I got caught in my memories

'Cause they never fail to prove

Months before that night on the beach, my folks had cut the cord. Shrouded by their anxiety over my future, they couldn't see how my ability to combine words and melodies could keep me afloat. Stuck between the best of intentions and their parental practicality, they couldn't conceive the notion of me as a musician; a vessel capable of bringing the physical and spiritual world together.

"Either you go to college, or get out of the house." Their well-meaning, tough-love ultimatum left me with few options. Do I entrust my future to my convictions and experience actual eviction from my home? Or do I give up my dream, my heavenly calling, and experience life vicariously through the biographies of history class?

Needless to say, my choice was met with the slam of the front door. And in the earthshaking wake of its closing, I was left on my own.

Alone, on the threshold between my parents' home and the world, part of me felt like shouting "I'll show you!" But as I walked away, with my guitar over my shoulder, I couldn't help but wonder if I had made the right choice—for the right reason. And fighting the desire to look back, I instead looked up. "Please, show me."

I felt like a fish out of water. My regular routine disappeared overnight, and my comfort zone was nowhere to be found. I was outside of my normal life; forced to depend not on my family, but my faith.

Although I was without any visible means of support, I managed to put a roof over my head, thanks to the generosity of some unexpected friends. And the worry of putting food on the table was lessened with the job I found in the local boat-yard, power-washing the hulls of ships. Self-sufficiency wasn't easy, but the struggle somehow strengthened the bond between me and the guys in my band. The challenge even brought my long-time girlfriend, Cortni, closer.

I was constantly fighting the undertow. When I wasn't cleaning barnacles off the underbellies of ships, I was on the road with the band, playing every weekend gig we could find. It didn't matter how far we had to travel, or how small our audience, our focus was on the message in the music. But getting that message out there was like trying to launch a barge at low tide. Despite how hard we rowed, we were going nowhere, very slowly.

Something was weighing us down, holding us back. Was it something in the music or in our presentation? Or was I dragging an anchor unaware?

I'm insecure and incomplete

It's a stinging point of truth

As with all stories of self-examination, the pivotal moment arrived when I least expected it. After an eternity of weekend concerts, our band somehow caught the attention of a record label. It seems that after hearing only a few stanzas of our repertoire, the powers-that-be were willing to consider what my folks had struggled to comprehend.

I didn't know whether to laugh or cry. Most musicians would not readily admit their need for a record deal, but it had always been my dream. A contract with a label would give the music and the band a visible platform, and provide the kind of behind-the-scenes support that every independent ensemble struggles to attain.

The answer seemed obvious. Finally! Our message of divine hope had the opportunity to reach the masses. Finally! We had a potential partner in our quest to declare the wonders of God. We could—*wait a second!*

Although the solution to our struggle seemed to float before me, like an unexpected life preserver, a sudden, sinking question engulfed me: If our music is about dependence on God, why am I leaning on a record deal, instead of Heaven's provision? Was this the right thing to do, for the right reason?

Fighting the desire to look ahead at our potential future, I looked up instead. "Please, show me."

But I'm not running from you anymore

I'm not running from you anymore, no

Not anymore

Now, beached on my island refuge, I sat waiting for the voice of God; not knowing if I was on the shore of launching a career or languishing on the outer banks of nowhere.

The longer I sat in the sand, the more I realized that I had been on this self-examining, soul-searching quest my whole life. Although I had given myself to Christ years ago, it seemed I had spent every day since trying to figure out who it was I had willingly volunteered.

I felt like a boat snatched out of the water and placed in dry dock; my underbelly was exposed, revealing all of the barnacles in my life that needed scraping. I felt stuck; not just between the mainland and the vast Atlantic Ocean, but between dependence on the comforts of home and the independence of self-sufficiency. I was stranded, not just between the dusk and the dawn, but amid the perceptions others have of me and the Me I have yet to find. And all of that juxtaposed against the musician my family couldn't see and the record label's perception—the big decision I expected to hear . . . today.

As the sun continued to rise behind me, I sat in my own growing shadow, still in the dark. It seemed I had too many options—and too few.

If the record label says yes, should I agree? And if I accept their offer, am I doing so because it is the financially right thing to do, the spiritually prudent thing to do, or just the thing I've always dreamed of doing? "Please, show me."

I believe that when I call for you

You hear the plea for my rescue

And you lift me up above the world I know

As I sat in my own sandy shadow contemplating these things, a light began to dawn, along with the sun. In that glimmering instant I realized that all this time I had been living in the shadows—not my own, but the shadows of all those that have populated my world: my parents, my friends, my band, my girl. And it hit me that residing in their shadows was not a bad thing, but actually a blessing!

Sitting on that beach with the sun behind me, I saw that a shadow is created by something between it and the light. And if I have been living in the shadow of all those saints that God has put into my life, then they have been purposely placed there, between me and his guiding luminescence.

And I know that when I speak your name

You hear my voice and send your saints

To cover me in the shadow of angels

My parents' tough-love ultimatum set me on the course Heaven planned. My friends' unexpected offer to take me in was the protection God provided. My job on the dry docks not only put food on the table, but gave me a visual metaphor of God's cleansing power-wash. My band was God's provision to accomplish my musical calling. And Cortni, who would later become my wife, was the angelic helpmate, the confidant, the ever-present shadow God placed next to me.

The darkness we experience is just the shadow of Heaven's provision, on its direct journey to us, straight from God's luminescent throne. In the radiance of this discovery, I realized that it no longer mattered which way the big decision went today; for I found my answer in the shadow of the record label dilemma God provided. Sitting on my solitary stretch of sand, where all my explorations seem to begin and end, I spent a dark night inside myself and at dawn, I was shown the Light.

I will never find the best of me

Until I find myself in you

I'll find myself in you

Between depending on a record label or leaning on the One who never labels us despite our record; I made the right choice . . . for the right reason.

✣ PRAYER ✣

Let me always be a vessel capable of bringing the physical and spiritual world together. And when it feels like I have no visible means of support, remind me that if I seek your kingdom first, record deals and all these other things . . . will follow.

> ❝Ask and it will be given to you; seek and you will find.❞
>
> MATTHEW 7:7

In the Shadow of Angels

{ BY JASON ROY }

Sunrise on Sunset Beach
Finds me right where I watched
   it set
I spent the night inside myself
But I haven't found me yet

But I'm not running from you
   anymore
I'm not running from you
   anymore, no
Not anymore

'Cause I believe that when I call
   for you
You hear the plea for my rescue
And you lift me up above the world
   I know
And I know that when I speak
   your name
You hear my voice and send
   your saints
To cover me in the shadow of angels

I got caught in my memories
'Cause they never fail to prove
I'm insecure and incomplete
It's a stinging point of truth
So I will never find the best of me
Until I find myself in you
I'll find myself in you

ACKNOWLEDGMENTS

APRIL HEFNER, if you had not published "Alone in Times Square" in *CCM Magazine* those many years ago, this collection would not exist. Your decision may have altered the magazine's format for a moment, but that center spread continues to transform the composition of my life into an ongoing page turner. Thank you.

CINDY WILT, your early and energetic support of this crazy man's idea (the many phone calls, e-mails and gracious introductions made) is what got this project off the ground. I *still* owe you lunch.

CHRISTINE WINSLOW, an unexpected delight, your zealous, hyper-infectious endorsement of this project not only stirred the imaginations of all the right people, it kept me motivated, too. Thank you for being the overzealous publicist I never hired.

TO THOSE WHO HELPED ME CONNECT THE DOTS—Jim Chaffee, Jeralee Mathews, Amy Barker, Bubba Smith, Jim Houser, Kimberly Burleson, Greg Lucid, Rich "Dandy" Guider, Tori Taff, Wayne Kirkpatrick, and my in-house editor Gail Green—in more ways than I can count your intervention made the magic happen. It's not what you know, but who you know, and your assistance made me at least appear to know something. Thank you, all.

Special recognition goes to the Petersons: Tacey, Amanda, Lauren, and Michael. Inviting me into your beautiful home, allowing me to bunk up in your "Green" room, was a perk more valuable than the money saved. Your friendship and effortless inclusion into your family made my frequent overnighters in Nashville enjoyable (and a lot more frequent.)

The continual faith of old pals such as Dennis Williams, Stephen Bransford, David and Becky VanKoevering, Valera Daniels Hoskins, Carol Courtney, Tim and Denise Goodwin, Ron Martin, Kim Kreiner, Jim and Angie Korakis, and Merrill Moore, along with the support of new friends, Allen and Belinda Taylor, Darla Osborn Jackson and Tony Smith—you all made my task of writing less a solitary effort, and more a collaboration of encouragement.

To my family at Standard Publishing: Diane Stortz, your confidence and unwavering patience, despite the journey's twists and turns, is a testament to your strength and insight. You are the destination that found me; and I thank God for you. And to editor Laura Derico, my work has been commended into your capable hands. It is my prayer that you enjoyed your assignment and had very little—better yet, *nothing* to do.

Finally, to all the artists and composers that entrusted their deeply personal stories into my care, I am amazed by your insightful talent, honored by your confidence, humbled by the challenge, and truly in awe of the effects our collaborations are already having ... between the lines and spaces.